The Hadassah

EVERYDAY COOKBOOK

Daily Meals for the Contemporary Jewish Kitchen

The Hadassah

EVERYDAY COOKBOOK

Daily Meals for the Contemporary Jewish Kitchen

Leah Koenig
with Photography by Lucy Schaeffer
Foreword by Joan Nathan

UNIVERSE

Published by Universe Publishing
A Division of Rizzoli International Publications, Inc.
300 Park Avenue South
New York, NY 10010
www.rizzoliusa.com

All photographs © Lucy Schaeffer

© Copyright 2011 Universe Publishing

The following recipes were originally published on
www.MyJewishLearning.com and appear here with permission:
Apple Walnut Bread (page 42), Pear Compote (page 30),
Grilled Pineapple with Minted Raspberry Smash (page 191),
Orange Chocolate Macaroons (page 178) and Malabi with
Pistachios (page 184).

Botanical illustrations © vanias — fotolia.com

Editor: Libby Barnea
Project Editor: Melissa Veronesi
Book Design: Lori S. Malkin
Food Stylist: Simon Andrews
Prop Stylist: Dani Fisher

2011 2012 2013 2014 / 10 9 8 7 6 5 4 3 2 1

Printed in China

ISBN-13: 978-0-7893-2221-0

Library of Congress Catalog Control Number: 2010935641

❧✦❧ ACKNOWLEDGMENTS

Thank you to Libby Barnea and Alan Tigay at *Hadassah Magazine* and everyone else at Hadassah for entrusting me with this book. I can only hope that I have done justice to Hadassah's legacy of producing classic Jewish cookbooks. Libby, thank you especially for being such a supportive and thoughtful editor and co-recipe tester along the way.

❧ ❧ ❧

Special thanks to Adeena Sussman, *Hadassah Magazine*'s food columnist and one of my personal food heroes. Your influence graces every page.

❧ ❧ ❧

Thanks to Jim Muschett, Lori Malkin, Melissa Veronesi and everyone on the Rizzoli team for envisioning this book and helping to make it a reality.

❧ ❧ ❧

Thank you to Joan Nathan for contributing this book's foreword and for continuing to set the gold standard for exemplary, passionate food writing— Jewish and otherwise.

❧ ❧ ❧

Thank you to Nigel Savage, Cheryl Cook and the entire Hazon staff for fostering my love of food, farmers and Jewish life—and for encouraging my food-writing journey by putting me at the helm of The Jew & the Carrot blog for two years. Thanks also to my editors at the *Forward* and MyJewishLearning.com for giving me the regular opportunity to flex my recipe-developing muscles.

Thank you to chef Laura Frankel for being an inspiring role model and for giving me my first taste of the cookbook world.

◆ ◆ ◆

Many thanks to the following like-minded cooks who contributed recipes to this cookbook: Rivka Friedman, whose food blog Not Derby Pie is a regular inspiration; Elisheva Margulies, a fellow sustainable foodie and founder of the natural foods service Eat with Eli; Julie Negrin, a nutritionist, cooking instructor and author of *Easy Meals to Cook with Kids*; Gayle Squires, who writes about all things kosher and delicious on the blog Kosher Camembert; and Sandy (Stollar) Leibowitz—friend and founder of The Kosher Tomato chef services.

◆ ◆ ◆

Thank you to all of my friends who offered recipes and advice from their own everyday kitchens: Julie Dawson, who introduced me to Romanian Jewish delicacies; Daniel and Dalit Horn, Dan Steingart and Rachel Kort, and Ellen Smith Ahearn. Extra thanks to Devra Ferst and Anna Hanau for helping me throw a delicious recipe-tasting party—and to everyone who came, ate and gave helpful feedback.

◆ ◆ ◆

Lucy Schaeffer, Simon Andrews, Dani Fisher, Shane Walsh and Madeline Hunnewell—thank you for letting me tag along while you styled and photographed the gorgeous pictures that accompany the recipes in this book.

◆ ◆ ◆

Thank you to my brother, Seth Koenig, and my parents, Richard and Carol Koenig, for supporting and loving me through every adventure. Special thanks to my mom for graciously opening up her recipe file, helping to test recipes and providing me with a model for healthy, love-filled everyday cooking.

◆ ◆ ◆

Rena, Chaim, Temim, Ora and Dasi Fruchter—thank you for welcoming me to your family and sharing your joyous Shabbat table time and again.

◆ ◆ ◆

And finally to my husband, Yoshie Fruchter, thank you for your constant support, love and good appetite—and for providing the soundtrack to my life.

✂◆✂ CONTENTS

*Granola, egg dishes, yogurt parfait,
smoothies, quick breads and muffins
to jumpstart the morning.*

*Green salads, main-course salads
and salatim-style spreads plus fresh
dressings.*

Sandwiches and Pizzas

*Inspired sandwiches
and pizzas for a quick
lunch or dinner.*

Soups and Stews

*Quick-simmering soups and
hearty stews that warm body
and soul.*

Sides

*Vegetable, pasta, rice and
grain dishes that tastefully
round out any table.*

Mains 138

Simple and nourishing chicken,
beef and fish dishes, vegetarian
mains, casseroles and egg suppers.

Sweets 170

Sumptuous desserts that
come together in no time.

Anytime Snacks 196

Nibbles and drinks to
delight guests or curl up
with on the couch.

⊲◆⊳ FOREWORD

by Joan Nathan

Although I can't recall when I first heard the name Hadassah, my earliest real memory of the Women's Zionist Organization of America comes from the 1970s, when I was in my twenties, working as a foreign press attaché for the legendary Teddy Kollek, who served 28 years as mayor of Jerusalem. Teddy, as everyone called him, filled me in on the importance of the organization before a delegation of Hadassah women arrived. "If you think I am your boss, you are wrong," he said. "It is the Hadassah ladies who run Jerusalem."

◆ ◆ ◆

Not exactly, but he truly admired the intelligence and tenacity of Hadassah volunteers and deeply appreciated the contributions they made to all the people of Jerusalem. Personally, women like Esther Gottesman, Rose Halprin and Miriam Freund-Rosenthal were great mentors to me.

And in those days in Jerusalem, daily food was extremely basic. Eating out at the very few upscale restaurants was considered a capitalist venture. Most people ate simple foods like hummus, turkey schnitzel and rice for lunch—the main meal of the day—with yogurt, cottage cheese or other dairy food accompanied by lots of vegetables for breakfast and dinner.

◆ ◆ ◆

But Hadassah is basically an American organization with American appetites and American food traditions. As I look over the past almost 100 years of Hadassah and the many Hadassah fund-raising cookbooks in my library, several things stand out. The women, like everyone else in this country, wanted to do it all: work, volunteer and still put healthy, good food on the table every day. Like everyone else, they sometimes fell for convenience foods: canned salmon made into croquettes or patties for Thursday night dinner or, for some variety, that wonderful American invention, tuna casserole made from canned mushroom soup, canned tuna and crumbled saltines or Corn Flakes on top. Some would eat Jell-O salads that could be made ahead, others cooked hamburger steak and still others heated up boxed macaroni and cheese. So ingrained in our lives were convenience foods that when I started to make macaroni and cheese from scratch, my children rebelled!

◆ ◆ ◆

My second major memory of Hadassah, from 1996, is of a young woman enrolled in the culinary arts department of what was then called Hadassah College of Technology, today Hadassah College Jerusalem. She was assisting the Michelin three-star French chef Pierre Troisgros in preparing one of the courses in a feast to celebrate the 3,000th anniversary of Jerusalem. They were sitting at a table plucking tarragon leaf by leaf to garnish a dish of eggplant and snapper from the Red Sea. This was clearly upscale food, the kind that dazzles: a 12-course kosher meal prepared by 7 three-star chefs, a meal I was covering for *The New York Times*.

◆ ◆ ◆

That dinner is a great example of "dress-up food," what I consider the first tier in my three-category system of classifying food today. Chefs in upscale restaurants all over the world are trying to tantalize customers with this fare. We watch the recipes being made while exercising at the gym. We make reservations to dine at the expensive restaurants. We try to impress guests at our own dinner parties with these wondrous novelties.

◆ ◆ ◆

The second category is traditional family food. We eat these foods on holidays and the Sabbath, pulling out timeworn recipes that say, "this is our family." One of my favorite American recipes, gleaned from a North Shore Chicago Hadassah cookbook, is Lick Your Fingers Kugel with caramelized pecans at the bottom of the tube pan, which I included in *Jewish Cooking in America*. Recipes like this elicit memories, laughter, stories and the binding together of generations. Hadassah cookbooks are filled with these recipes.

◆ ◆ ◆

But this Hadassah cookbook tackles the third category, which I consider the most challenging: everyday food. Times have changed and so have our lifestyles, our expectations and our thirst for exotic and healthy food. As the interest in organic, local and what I call "good food" is sweeping the country, boxed macaroni and cheese is no longer a desirable option. We want meals made from scratch but we still want them done without too much fuss.

♦ ♦ ♦

How lucky Hadassah is to have Leah Koenig, one of the rising stars in a new generation of Jewish food writers, compose this latest Hadassah cookbook. I had the honor of getting to know Leah when I invited her to take part in a gastronomic trip to Israel I organized for culinary journalists. She is smart, lovely and modest. The recipes Leah showcases in this cookbook are simple, delicious, good for us and attuned to our times. It is a natural fit that Hadassah, the largest Jewish woman's organization in America and with a legacy of producing beloved cookbooks, would be the force behind such a collection.

♦ ♦ ♦

Lastly, in cooking with your families, I urge you to involve everyone in the process: your children, your partner, even your grandparents if they live with you. As you are shopping, picking vegetables from the garden or stirring a soup, you will have the chance to talk—cell phones off, please!—and when you finally sit down to eat, everyone will appreciate the outcome.

❧ **JOAN NATHAN** is the author of 8 Jewish award-winning cookbooks. Her most recent book is *Quiches, Kugels, and Couscous: My Search for Jewish Cooking in France* (Knopf).

❧◆❧ INTRODUCTION

by Leah Koenig

L et's get this out of the way at the start: I am not a professional cook. I have no degree from culinary school hanging on my wall, and no hours logged as an overworked restaurant line chef. And although I grew up in a house where family dinners were a priority, I did not learn how to make anything beyond grilled cheese and chocolate chip cookies until college.

◆ ◆ ◆

I got my first taste of the pleasures of the stove while living in the Environmental Studies house (aka "the hippie co-op") during my senior year at Middlebury College in Middlebury, Vermont. There, my 16 scrappy, unshaven housemates and I were in charge of making dinner for ourselves—and any other students who dropped by—night after night. At first I watched, spellbound, as my housemates casually whipped up simple, honest meals— steaming pots of chili, giant fresh salads and hearty casseroles—that left everyone feeling cared for and satisfied. By the end of the semester, I had absorbed some tricks of the trade. At the very least, I could dice an onion, make a decent omelet and cobble together a homemade salad dressing without breaking into too much of a sweat. During that year I also got my first glimpse of the true power of food and community, and the immense satisfaction I felt in transforming a pile of ingredients into a nourishing meal.

◆ ◆ ◆

Since then, my love of cooking has swelled like rising bread dough. Good fortune has also guided me toward many exceptional food experiences: from a stint working on an organic vineyard in Italy, to running a national Community Supported Agriculture program for the Jewish environmental organization, Hazon (and collaborating with many inspiring farmers, chefs and food enthusiasts along the way), to branching out as a professional food writer (who would have thought!) and marrying a wonderful person who taught me about *kashrut* and the joy of cooking with and for family. So while I am still by no means a gourmet chef, I am an enthusiastic home cook who counts feeding others as one of my greatest passions.

◆ ◆ ◆

I am not alone. Combining a reverence for books and an obsession with food, Jews could easily be considered the "people of the cookbook." Our culinary tradition is rich with time-tested dishes—matza ball soup, gefilte fish, cholent, brisket, bourekas—that we turn to on Shabbat and the holidays to imbue our celebrations with meaning and the flavors of home. Fittingly, the Jewish cookbook canon is filled with treasured, well-worn books that capture these recipes and make them accessible to our contemporary kitchens.

But Shabbat and the holidays only make up a fraction of the meals we eat during the year. After the challah crumbs are brushed from the table and the wine glasses tucked back in the cabinet, there are still a mind-boggling number of breakfasts, lunches and dinners to sort out. It's enough to inspire a small fit of culinary panic. And while potato kugel and honey cake are undeniably delicious, you would be hard-pressed to find a nutritionist recommending them as part of a regular healthy diet. This Jewish cookbook, then, takes a slightly different focus than most—tackling the everyday question, "what's to eat?"

◆ ◆ ◆

We all know what it feels like to come home from a long day and open the refrigerator for inspiration—only to end up eating leftover takeout or microwaving a frozen meal. There are as many everyday realities as there are people. But despite our best intentions, most of us simply have less time to spend crafting homemade, nourishing meals for our friends and family than we would like. It doesn't have to be this way. No matter how harried things get, with a bit of forethought and guidance, simple, fresh and truly delicious kosher meals can become a fixture of your daily routine.

◆ ◆ ◆

Fortunately, now is an incredibly exciting time in the world of cooking and eating. Farmers' markets in cities and towns across the country overflow with gorgeous, locally grown and organic produce. Meanwhile, artisan-made cheeses and breads, sustainable meat and high-quality wine are increasingly available and increasingly kosher-certified. And on the

other end of the spectrum, the global marketplace has brought a world of flavors and products—from kosher mascarpone cheese to sheets of Japanese nori and gluten-free pastas—to our kitchens. Throughout history, daily Jewish eating habits have mirrored those of their non-Jewish neighbors, and today is no exception. A typical weeknight dinner in an American Jewish home is now just as likely to include Mexican, Italian or Asian-inspired dishes as something more explicitly Jewish.

◆ ◆ ◆

This book celebrates exactly this kind of seasonal, globally inspired cooking while maintaining the nurturing spirit and sensibility of the traditional Jewish kitchen. The recipes themselves offer a little something for everyone—recent college graduates finding their way in a new city and newlyweds settling into their new lives; busy professionals who enjoy spending Sunday afternoons tinkering in the kitchen and new parents who are redefining the notion of "short on time"; families looking for healthy dishes to feed the whole gang and empty nesters rediscovering the joys of cooking for a smaller crowd.

◆ ◆ ◆

So when you are looking for inspiration for an on-the-go breakfast or casual brunch, a soup-and-salad lunch or a divine (yet down-to-earth) dinner without the fuss, *The Hadassah Everyday Cookbook* has you covered.

❧◆❧ A FEW NOTES ON USING THIS BOOK. . .
and general kitchen satisfaction

◆ THE ICONS

Planning a meal? Look for the little **Ⓓ** (Dairy), **Ⓜ** (Meat) and **Ⓟ** (Pareve) letters after each recipe introduction for a quick reference to that dish's kosher status.

◆ MAKE TIME WORK FOR YOU

Time can be a home cook's greatest ally, if you use it well. Before pulling ingredients from your refrigerator and pantry, take a minute to plot your plan of attack. Do any of the dishes you are making require baking or simmering time? Start with those and once they are cooking in the oven or bubbling on the stovetop, use that time to prep other dishes, make a salad or set the table. By the time the oven timer dings, the rest of dinner will be ready.

◆ DON'T OVERDOSE ON CONVENIENCE

Today's supermarkets are stocked with every imaginable convenience food from bottled lemon juice to canned soups and frozen piecrust. But while these culinary shortcuts do decrease cooking times, many of them come loaded with added salt, sugar or preservatives and lack the depth of flavor found in their fresh counterparts. Think about it—when was the last time canned peaches made you swoon like a perfect fresh peach?

Still, when it comes to everyday cooking, time is of the essence and sometimes that frozen piecrust makes all the difference. So go fresh whenever possible and save the best convenience ingredients—things like frozen vegetables, jarred tomato sauce, canned beans and brownie mix—for when you really need them.

◆ DEVELOP YOUR CHOPS

The most important thing any home cook can do to speed up cooking times and gain confidence in the kitchen is to learn basic knife skills. So invest in a good set of knives and treat yourself to a knife course at your local Jewish Community Center or cooking school (or search the term "knife skills" on YouTube and watch a few instructional videos). Before long, you will be able to tackle any pile of fresh vegetables with speed and conviction. And remember, a sharp knife is safer than a dull one, so keep your blades honed.

◆ STOCK YOUR PANTRY

It almost goes without saying, but a well-stocked pantry is a crucial aspect of simple, everyday cooking. When you are at the grocery store ask yourself: Are there certain items—dried pasta or rice, spices or herbs, olive oil or tahini paste, chicken broth or bulbs of garlic—that you tend to use a lot in your cooking? Buy a few extra of each and stash them in your cupboard so that you don't end up halfway through a recipe only to realize you are out of a crucial ingredient.

The same logic applies to kitchen gear. There is no need to buy every kitchen gadget on the market, but equipping yourself with some essentials—an immersion blender, a zester, a sturdy whisk, a cast-iron pan and grill pan or whatever gear you use most frequently—will ensure you have all the tools you need to handle dinner with grace and ease.

◆ CHOOSE LOCAL AND ORGANIC— AT LEAST SOMETIMES

If eating all organic or locally grown food feels unrealistic for your budget, pick 5–10 groceries to prioritize—especially milk, eggs, meat and certain thin-skinned produce like peaches, berries, bell peppers, grapes, potatoes and leafy greens—and strive to buy organic and/or local every time. Boost your sustainable food count by shopping regularly at farmers' market (where you can ask questions about farmers' growing practices) or joining a Community Supported Agriculture program, which delivers just-picked local vegetables to your neighborhood every week. Your meals will not only taste fresher, but will also be safer for you, your family and the earth.

◆ FOLLOW THE RULES—ONLY IF YOU WANT TO

One of the most common statements you hear from experienced cooks is, "Oh, I don't really use recipes—I just cook by feel." While there is something magical about the notion of whimsically tossing ingredients into a pot until a dish tastes right, this sort of improvisational cooking can be intimidating to newer cooks.

The recipes in this book are written with clear, straightforward directions to guide all cooks toward a delicious dish or meal, regardless of their previous kitchen experience. So newbies take heart, then take a deep breath and give them a shot. As for the old pros, think of these recipes as flavors and ideas to riff off of—basic structures to which you can add or substitute ingredients to your heart's (and taste buds') desire. The most important thing is to feel in charge—and at home—in the kitchen.

A Blessing for the Cook

"Blessed are You
Creator of the world
Who brings forth fruit from the Earth.
Blessed are You,
Who gives us knowledge of cooking, and time to cook
And who has blessed us with the need for nourishment
so that we can fully understand Your gifts.
May it be Your will
That the food that I cook
Brings nourishment, fulfillment and happiness
to those who eat it
And bring honor to the land and all the people that
make this meal possible."

—LEAH KOENIG AND ANNA HANAU,
WRITTEN FOR HAZON'S BEIT MIDRASH ON JEWS,
FOOD AND CONTEMPORARY LIFE (2006)

BREAKFASTS AND BREADS

Breakfasts and

B reakfast is a meal of many moods. Sometimes it is frenzied—a cup of coffee and toast eaten on the go, or a bowl of cereal gobbled, bleary-eyed, before work. Other times it is a sumptuous and drawn-out affair, accompanied by the newspaper and stretching lazily toward lunchtime. Sometimes it is sweet, other times savory; sometimes it is decadent and other times light and refreshing.

♦ ♦ ♦

What binds all of breakfast's moods together is that they represent the first food we put in our bodies each day. Nutritionists and food experts often stress the importance of gathering at the dinner table, but what if we applied this wisdom to the morning? How might our days be different, and possibly even better, if we took the time to savor breakfast or share it with family and friends?

Breads

After a long day of abstaining from food on Yom Kippur, Jews literally break the fast together. These meals, with their elaborate fruit platters, quiches and bagel spreads, are celebratory and tinged with an extra sense of gratefulness for the return to physical nourishment. In that sense, Yom Kippur's break fast is an ideal model for every breakfast.

◆ ◆ ◆

Of course, the reality of our morning routines can make having breakfast together, or even having it at all, a challenge. But no matter how rushed things feel, setting aside 15 minutes to eat—before checking e-mail or flipping on the television—is ultimately a satisfying and valuable way to start the morning.

◆ ◆ ◆

The Jewish food canon is home to many breakfast classics, from thick-cut challah French toast to eggy matza brie and, the most iconic of all, bagels spread with cream cheese and topped with lox. The recipes in this section pay homage to these traditional tastes while celebrating the many moods of breakfast. There's a **Blackberry Mint Smoothie** *(page 48)* and **Cardamom-Scented Oatmeal** *(page 46)* that come together in the time it takes to brush your teeth, and make-ahead **Granola with Tahini** *(page 47)* to stir into yogurt at home or the office. There are **Maple Walnut Muffins** *(page 46)* and slices of **Honeyed Pumpkin Bread** *(page 41)* to smother with jam, and decadent **Smoked Salmon Scrambled Eggs** *(page 36)* and **Blueberry Cornmeal Pancakes** *(page 33)* to linger over on the weekend. So whatever mood your morning takes, make it a delicious one.

PAGES 26–27: *Chocolate Apricot Scones, recipe, page 42; Raspberry Oatmeal Muffins, recipe, page 45; Apple Walnut Bread, recipe, page 42*

❈❖❈ Challah French Toast with Pear Compote

In his book *Jewish Home Cooking: Yiddish Recipes Revisited*, Arthur Schwartz writes that challah French toast was popularized in the 1950s and '60s by Brooklyn restaurants like Wolfie's and Cookie's. This version tops the classic with a ginger-spiced pear compote. Ⓓ **Serves 4**

FOR TOAST:
5 large eggs
1 cup milk
1 teaspoon sugar
Pinch of salt
4 tablespoons unsalted butter or
    vegetable oil
8 thick, 3/4-inch slices of challah

FOR COMPOTE:
1 large or 2 small Bosc pears,
    finely chopped
1 tablespoon agave nectar
    (or maple syrup)
1/2 teaspoon ground ginger
1 tablespoon water
1/2 teaspoon crystallized ginger,
    finely chopped (optional)

1 ◆ In a medium bowl, whisk together eggs, milk, sugar and salt. Pour mixture into a 9 x 13-inch baking dish. Melt 1 tablespoon butter in a nonstick pan or griddle until bubbling but not brown.

2 ◆ Meanwhile, submerge two slices of challah in the egg mixture, one at a time, until well coated on each side. Fry egged bread for approximately 2 minutes on each side until golden brown. Keep slices warm on a baking sheet set in a 200-degree oven while you finish cooking the other slices, adding more butter to the skillet as needed. Serve topped with maple syrup or pear compote.

3 ◆ *Make compote:* Combine all ingredients in a small saucepan and cook over low heat, stirring regularly, until the pears soften and soak up the fragrant ginger liquid, 10–12 minutes. Adjust by adding small amounts of water or agave nectar or maple syrup until you reach your desired consistency.

Challah French Toast with Pear Compote ▶

Blueberry Cornmeal Pancakes

S ay goodbye to pancake mix—these fruit-flecked beauties only
take minutes to prepare. ⓓ **Makes about 10 pancakes**

1/2 cup all-purpose flour
1/2 cup cornmeal
1/2 teaspoon salt
1 teaspoon baking powder
1/2 teaspoon baking soda
1/4 cup sugar
1 cup milk

1/8 teaspoon cider vinegar
2 large eggs
1 tablespoon butter, melted
1 cup blueberries, fresh or thawed
frozen
Butter or cooking spray for pan

1 ◆ In a medium bowl, mix together flour, cornmeal, salt, baking powder, baking soda and sugar; set aside.

2 ◆ In a large bowl, whisk together milk, vinegar, eggs and melted butter. Pour dry mixture into wet and stir until just incorporated. (Do not over mix or your pancakes will be tough—lumps at this stage are O.K.)

3 ◆ Heat a large nonstick pan or griddle over medium heat; melt a little butter in the bottom or coat lightly with cooking spray. Ladle scant 1/4 cup batter into the pan for each pancake and sprinkle a few blueberries onto each pancake. (If using thawed frozen blueberries, toss with 1 teaspoon of flour before adding to pancakes.)

4 ◆ Cook until the tops of the pancakes are speckled with bubbles. Flip and cook until underside is lightly browned.

5 ◆ Serve immediately or keep pancakes warm on a baking sheet set in a 200-degree oven until you finish cooking the rest. Serve with maple syrup and butter.

◀ *Blueberry Cornmeal Pancakes*

Whole Wheat Granola Pancakes

This hearty breakfast dish is inspired by the granola pancakes served at Louis Family Restaurant, a vegetarian-friendly greasy spoon in Providence, Rhode Island. ⓓ **Serves 4**

1 cup whole wheat flour	*1 tablespoon unsalted butter,*
1/2 cup all-purpose flour	*melted*
3 tablespoons sugar	*2 large eggs*
1 1/2 teaspoons baking powder	*1/2 teaspoon vanilla*
Dash of nutmeg	*1/2 cup granola, store-bought or*
1/2 teaspoon salt	*homemade (recipe, page 47)*
1 1/2 cups milk	*Butter or cooking spray for pan*

1 ◆ In a medium bowl, mix together flours, sugar, baking powder, nutmeg and salt: set aside.

2 ◆ In a large bowl, whisk together milk, butter, eggs and vanilla. Incorporate dry mixture into wet and stir until just combined. Gently fold in the granola.

3 ◆ Heat a nonstick pan or griddle over medium heat; melt a little butter on the bottom or coat lightly with cooking spray. Ladle approximately 1/4 cup batter into the pan for each pancake and cook until the tops of the pancakes are speckled with bubbles. Flip pancakes and cook until undersides are lightly browned.

4 ◆ Serve immediately or keep pancakes warm on a baking sheet in a 200-degree oven until you finish cooking the rest. Serve with fresh fruit, maple syrup and butter.

Mushroom Leek Omelet with Parmesan

Omelets are the perfect way to feed a crowd fast. This one features the tasty duo of leeks softened in butter and savory crimini mushrooms. ⓓ **Serves 4–6**

2 tablespoons butter or olive oil	*10 large eggs*
1 small leek, thinly sliced	*1/4 cup milk*
Salt and freshly ground black pepper	*1/2 cup grated Parmesan*
1/2 cup crimini mushrooms, sliced	*cheese*

1 ◆ Heat butter or oil in a skillet over medium-low heat. Add leek and a pinch of salt and sauté, stirring occasionally, until leeks soften slightly, about 7 minutes. Add mushrooms and cook until soft, about 5 minutes.

2 ◆ Meanwhile, beat eggs in a large bowl and combine with milk, salt and pepper to taste; whisk thoroughly to combine.

3 ◆ Pour egg mixture over leek and mushrooms; cover skillet and cook until eggs are set, 8–10 minutes. Remove from heat and divide omelet between plates. Sprinkle individual portions with Parmesan just before serving.

Horseradish Omelet

Passover's favorite bitter herb adds a surprising (and delightful) kick to a cheese omelet. ⓘ **Serves 4–6**

⇒TIP Adjust the amount of prepared white horseradish in this omelet to taste.

2 tablespoons olive oil
3 scallions, chopped
10 large eggs
1/4 cup milk
Salt and freshly ground black pepper

4 1/2 teaspoons prepared white horseradish
1/2 cup shredded white cheddar cheese

1 ◆ Heat oil in a skillet over medium-low heat. Add scallions and sauté, stirring occasionally, until slightly browned, about 5 minutes.

2 ◆ Meanwhile, beat eggs in a large bowl and combine with milk, salt and pepper to taste and horseradish; whisk thoroughly to combine.

3 ◆ Pour egg mixture over scallions; cover skillet and cook until eggs are set, 8–10 minutes. When eggs are done, uncover skillet and sprinkle cheese evenly over omelet. Turn off heat and re-cover until cheese melts.

Smoked Salmon Scrambled Eggs

These eggs feature the smoky, salty taste of a Jewish breakfast icon: lox. For over-the-top Brooklyn flavor, spoon them onto a lightly toasted everything bagel. Ⓓ **Serves 4**

1/2 cup sour cream	*Salt and freshly ground black*
4 tablespoons chopped dill plus	*pepper*
more for garnish	*1 tablespoon olive oil*
8 large eggs	*Half a medium onion, minced*
3 tablespoons milk	*4 ounces smoked salmon,*
	roughly chopped

1 ◆ Combine sour cream and dill in a small bowl and set aside in the refrigerator. Whisk together eggs, milk and salt and pepper to taste in a medium bowl and set aside.

2 ◆ Heat oil in a skillet over medium heat. Add onion and cook until translucent, 5–7 minutes. Add eggs and cook, stirring with a rubber spatula, until eggs hold together but are still slightly soft, about 5 minutes. Add smoked salmon and continue cooking 1–2 minutes until eggs are firm.

3 ◆ Divide eggs onto serving plates and dollop sour cream mixture on top. Sprinkle with reserved dill and more pepper.

Smoked Salmon Scrambled Eggs ▶

⋈◆⋈ Salsa and Cheddar Home Fries

Bring the diner home with these crispy, gooey home fries. They taste great alongside salad greens drizzled with olive oil and fresh lemon juice, and topped with a poached or fried egg. Ⓓ **Serves 4–6**

4 russet potatoes (about 2 pounds), cut into 1/4-inch pieces
Salt and freshly ground black pepper, salt divided
1/4 cup vegetable oil

2 onions, chopped
1/2 teaspoon garlic powder
1/2 cup salsa
1/2 cup grated cheddar cheese
1 tablespoon chopped flat-leaf parsley (optional)

1 ◆ Put the potato pieces in a medium saucepan and cover with cold salted water by about 2 inches. Bring to a boil, lower the heat and simmer until just tender, 6–8 minutes. Drain and set potatoes aside.

2 ◆ Meanwhile, heat oil in a large nonstick pan or cast-iron skillet over medium heat. Add onion and cook until just browned, about 7 minutes. Add cooked potatoes, season with garlic powder and salt and pepper to taste and cook until crispy and browned, stirring occasionally, 8–10 minutes.

3 ◆ Turn off heat; stir in the salsa and cheddar and cover to allow the cheese to melt. Served topped with parsley, if desired.

⋈◆⋈ Mushroom, Leek and Cheese Strata

Serve this cheesy, herb-speckled strata as a centerpiece at Sunday brunch. Ⓓ **Serves 6**

4 tablespoons unsalted butter, divided
2 medium leeks, thinly sliced
1 1/2 cups crimini mushrooms, thinly sliced
2 tablespoons chopped fresh basil or 1 teaspoon dried

Salt and freshly ground black pepper
6 large eggs
2 1/4 cups milk
1 loaf sturdy bread, cubed (day-old is fine)
1 cup grated cheddar cheese
1 1/2 cups grated Parmesan cheese

1 ◆ Melt 2 tablespoons butter in a large pan over medium-high heat. Add leeks and sauté until soft, 7–8 minutes. Add mushrooms, basil and salt and pepper to taste and continue to cook another 5 minutes. Set aside to cool.

2 ◆ Meanwhile, whisk eggs and milk together in a large bowl. Season with additional salt and pepper to taste.

3 ◆ Spread a layer of bread cubes evenly in the bottom of a buttered 9 x 13-inch baking dish (you should have some cubes left over). Spread vegetable mixture over bread and top with cheddar. Pour egg mixture over and top with remaining bread cubes. Press bread lightly into egg mixture; dot top with remaining 2 tablespoons of butter. Cover and refrigerate at least 2 hours or overnight.

4 ◆ Preheat oven to 350 degrees. Uncover strata and sprinkle evenly with Parmesan. Bake until strata is browned, 50–60 minutes. Let stand 5 minutes before cutting.

❈◆❈ Portobello Mushroom Toast

Take a break from your daily toast and jam routine with this savory, chili-spiced mushroom sauté that you can make in just minutes. ⓘ **Serves 4**

2 tablespoons olive oil
3 shallots, finely chopped
Salt
5 portobello mushrooms, stemmed and cut into 1/4-inch dice*
2 cloves garlic, chopped
1/2 teaspoon dried thyme

1/4 cup heavy cream
4 slices hearty multigrain bread, toasted
Freshly ground black pepper
2 teaspoons chili powder or smoked paprika

✻TIP *If you prefer, swap 2 cups of crimini mushrooms for the portobellos.*

1 ◆ Heat oil in a skillet over medium heat. Add shallots and a pinch of salt and sauté, stirring occasionally, until shallots soften, about 6 minutes. Add mushrooms, garlic and thyme and cook, stirring occasionally, until mushrooms brown slightly, 5–7 minutes. Add cream and cook, stirring continuously, until cream is incorporated, about 3 minutes.

2 ◆ Remove pan from heat. Divide toast onto four plates and top each with a heaping scoop of the mushroom mixture. Top with pepper to taste and a sprinkling of chili powder or paprika.

Radish Breakfast Sandwich with Caraway Butter

This French classic has just a hint of added Jewish flavor thanks to the rye bread and caraway butter. Ⓓ Ⓟ **Serves 4**

5 tablespoons butter or non-hydrogenated margarine, softened

1/4 teaspoon caraway seeds, toasted

4 slices rye bread (toasted, if desired)

5–6 radishes (any color), thinly sliced

Sea salt

◆ Combine butter or margarine and caraway seeds in a small bowl and stir until seeds are incorporated. Spread caraway butter evenly on bread slices. Top each slice with a layer of radishes and sprinkle lightly with sea salt to taste.

Honeyed Pumpkin Bread

Spread with peanut butter or fruit preserves, a slice of this bread makes the perfect on-the-go breakfast. Bake a loaf on Sunday night and enjoy delicious breakfasts during the week. This bread doubles as a delicious pareve dessert. Ⓟ **Makes 1 loaf**

1 cup all-purpose flour

1/2 cup whole wheat flour

1/2 teaspoon salt

1/2 cup sugar

1 teaspoon baking soda

1 cup canned pumpkin purée

1/2 cup vegetable oil

1/2 cup honey

1 large egg, lightly beaten

1/4 cup water

1/2 teaspoon nutmeg

1/2 teaspoon cinnamon

1/2 cup walnuts, chopped

1 ◆ Preheat oven to 350 degrees. Combine the flours, salt, sugar and baking soda in a small bowl. Mix the pumpkin, oil, honey, egg, water and spices together in a separate bowl. Add the dry ingredients to the wet and mix with a wooden spoon until just incorporated. Fold in the nuts.

2 ◆ Pour into a greased 9 x 5 x 3-inch loaf pan. Bake for 50–60 minutes until a toothpick inserted in the center of the loaf comes out clean. Cool on a rack before serving.

◀ *Radish Breakfast Sandwich with Caraway Butter*

Apple Walnut Bread, photo page 27

Apple Walnut Bread

This super moist, nutritious quick bread is reminiscent of a Rosh Hashana apple cake. For a twist, pour the batter into cupcake or muffin trays. **P** Makes 2 loaves

2 cups all-purpose flour
1 cup whole wheat flour
1 teaspoon salt
1 teaspoon cinnamon
1 teaspoon baking soda
2 cups sugar
1 cup vegetable oil
2 teaspoons vanilla extract

3 large eggs
3 cups Golden Delicious or Granny Smith apples, peeled, cored and chopped
1 cup walnuts, chopped
1/4 cup ground flax seeds (flax seed meal)
Turbinado sugar (raw sugar; for sprinkling on top)

1 ◆ Preheat oven to 350 degrees. Combine both flours, salt, cinnamon and baking soda in a medium bowl and set aside. In a second bowl, mix together sugar, oil and vanilla.

2 ◆ Add eggs one at a time to wet mixture and stir to combine. Pour wet mixture into the dry ingredients and stir until thoroughly combined. Fold in apples and walnuts (the batter will be very thick).

3 ◆ Lightly grease two loaf pans and spread half of the batter into each. Sprinkle the tops with a little sugar and bake for approximately one hour, or until a toothpick stuck in the middle of the cake comes out clean.

FLAX SEEDS

Flax (also called linseed) is an ancient whole grain whose seeds are an excellent source of fiber and omega-3 fatty acids. Whole and pre-ground flax seeds can be found in health food stores and are increasingly available at the supermarket.

Store flax in the freezer (like with nuts, the oil in the seeds can spoil if left in the pantry), and grind whole seeds as needed in a spice grinder or with an immersion blender. Sprinkle on ground flax to boost the nutritional profile of hot cereals, pancakes, baked goods and smoothies.

Chocolate Apricot Scones

Chocolate dipped apricots are a favorite Passover dessert. Here, they are reinvented in a non-Passover-friendly (but decidedly delicious) scone. **D** Makes 8–12 scones

1 1/2 cups all-purpose flour
3/4 cup whole wheat flour
1 tablespoon baking powder
1/4 cup sugar
1 teaspoon salt
1/2 cup (1 stick) cold butter, cut into pieces

1/2 cup dried apricots, diced
3/4 cup milk or semisweet chocolate chips
1 large egg
2/3 cup heavy cream, plus more for brushing

1 ◆ Preheat oven to 425 degrees. In a large bowl, combine the flours, baking powder, sugar and salt. Add the butter and, using your fingers, mix together until the mixture resembles coarse crumbs. Fold in the apricots and chocolate chips.

Chocolate Apricot Scones, photo page 26

2 ◆ Whisk the egg and cream together in a separate bowl, then add it to the dry mixture, stirring to combine. Turn the dough out onto a lightly floured surface and knead about 30 seconds, until it comes together. If the mixture feels too wet to manage, slowly add a little more flour.

3 ◆ Gently pat the dough into a ball, then flatten into a 1-inch thick disk. Slice disk into quarters, then cut each quarter in half or thirds, depending on desired scone size. Use a pastry brush to skim tops with a little extra cream and sprinkle with extra sugar, if desired.

4 ◆ Transfer scones to a baking sheet and bake for about 15 minutes, or until golden brown on the bottom and set on the top. Serve warm topped with butter or jam. Store leftover scones in an airtight container and reheat in the oven or toaster oven before serving.

◆◆◆ Cheddar and Chive Scones

Freshly grated cheddar cheese and chives pair perfectly in these savory breakfast scones. ① **Makes 8–12 scones**

1 1/2 cups all-purpose flour
3/4 cup whole wheat flour
1 tablespoon baking powder
1 tablespoon sugar
1 1/4 teaspoons salt
1/2 cup (1 stick) cold butter, cut into pieces

1/4 cup finely chopped fresh chives
1 cup grated sharp cheddar cheese
1 large egg
2/3 cup heavy cream, plus more for brushing

1 ◆ Preheat oven to 425 degrees. In a large bowl, combine the flours, baking powder, sugar and salt. Add the butter and, using your fingers, mix together until the mixture resembles coarse crumbs. Fold in the chives and cheddar.

2 ◆ Whisk the egg and cream together in a separate bowl, then add it to the dry mixture, stirring to combine. Turn the dough out onto a lightly floured surface and knead about 30 seconds, until it comes together. If the mixture feels too wet to manage, slowly add a little more flour.

3 ◆ Gently pat the dough into a ball, then flatten into a 1-inch thick disk. Slice disk into quarters, then cut each quarter in half or thirds, depending on desired scone size. Use a pastry brush to skim tops with a little extra cream.

4 ◆ Transfer scones to a baking sheet and bake for about 15 minutes, or until golden brown on the bottom and set on the top. Serve warm topped with butter. Store leftover scones in an airtight container and reheat in the oven or toaster oven before serving.

Raspberry Oatmeal Muffins

Studded with juicy raspberries and flecks of oatmeal, these muffins make any morning routine a little bit brighter. **Ⓓ Makes 12 muffins**

1 cup all-purpose flour
1 teaspoon baking powder
1/2 teaspoon baking soda
1/4 teaspoon nutmeg
1/2 teaspoon cinnamon
1/4 teaspoon salt
1/2 cup unsalted butter, melted

1/2 cup brown sugar, firmly packed
1 large egg, lightly beaten
1/2 cup milk
1 teaspoon vanilla extract
1 cup instant oats
1 cup fresh or thawed frozen
  raspberries

1 ◆ Preheat oven to 375 degrees. Line a cupcake tray with silicone or paper cupcake cups.

2 ◆ In a medium bowl, combine the flour, baking powder, baking soda, nutmeg, cinnamon and salt; set aside. In a large bowl or standing mixer, mix the butter and brown sugar until fully combined. Add egg, milk and vanilla to butter mixture and mix until thoroughly combined. Slowly add the dry ingredients to the wet and mix to combine; fold in the oats.

3 ◆ Fill each cupcake cup a little less than half way. Gently press a few raspberries into the batter and cover with more batter until the cups are 3/4 full. If desired, press a couple of raspberries into the top of each muffin.

4 ◆ Bake muffins for 18–20 minutes until brown and a tester inserted in the middle of one comes out clean. Set on a wire rack to cool.

◀ *Raspberry Oatmeal Muffins*

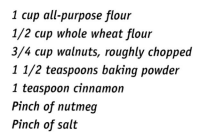

❊◆❊ Maple Walnut Muffins

The combination of the whole wheat flour and sweet banana in these muffins elevates their nutritional profile without sacrificing on taste. Ⓓ **Makes 12 muffins**

1 cup all-purpose flour
1/2 cup whole wheat flour
3/4 cup walnuts, roughly chopped
1 1/2 teaspoons baking powder
1 teaspoon cinnamon
Pinch of nutmeg
Pinch of salt

1/2 cup milk
1 large egg
1/3 cup maple syrup
1/3 cup vegetable oil
1 banana, mashed
1 teaspoon vanilla extract
Brown sugar for sprinkling

1 ◆ Preheat oven to 375 degrees. Line a cupcake tray with silicone or paper cupcake cups.

2 ◆ In a large bowl, mix together the flours, walnuts, baking powder, cinnamon, nutmeg and salt and set aside. In a medium bowl, whisk together milk, egg, maple syrup, oil, banana and vanilla. Pour wet mixture into the dry mixture and gently stir to combine.

3 ◆ Distribute the batter among the cupcake cups and sprinkle a little brown sugar on top of each. Bake for approximately 20 minutes, until a tester inserted in the middle of one comes out clean and the tops are lightly golden. Set on a wire rack to cool.

❊◆❊ Cardamom-Scented Oatmeal

Cold, dreary mornings are no match for a bowl of steaming, fragrant oatmeal studded with your favorite fixings. Ⓓ Ⓟ **Serves 4**

2 cups water
1 1/2 cups milk (or soy or almond milk)
1/4 teaspoon salt

1/2 teaspoon ground cardamom
1/2 teaspoon cinnamon
2 cups rolled oats (not instant)

1 ◆ Bring water, milk, salt and spices to a boil in a medium saucepan. Lower heat to medium, stir in the oats and cook 6–8 minutes, stirring occasionally, until thickened.

2 ◆ Garnish with any combination of the following (or add your own favorites): maple syrup, toasted pecans or walnuts, raisins, dried cherries, cranberries or apricots, granola, chopped apple or pear.

✕◆✕ Granola with Tahini

While tahini (ground sesame seed paste) is most often associated with hummus, in this dish it earns the moniker "peanut butter of the Middle East." Serve this sweet and nutty granola on top of yogurt (see **Greek Yogurt and Berry Parfait**, page 49) or as a crunchy pancake batter stir-in (see **Whole Wheat Granola Pancakes**, page 34). If desired, you can swap regular peanut butter or almond butter for the tahini. ℗ **Makes about 7 cups**

1/3 cup maple syrup
1/4 cup tahini
1/2 teaspoon salt
1 teaspoon cinnamon
2 1/2 cups rolled oats (not instant)
2/3 cup pumpkin seeds, salted or unsalted

2/3 cup sliced almonds
2/3 cup chopped pecans
2/3 cup raisins or cranberries
2 tablespoons crystallized ginger, chopped (optional)

1 ◆ Preheat oven to 325 degrees. In a small bowl, whisk together maple syrup, tahini, salt and cinnamon and set aside. In a large bowl, mix all remaining ingredients. Drizzle the syrup-tahini mixture over the seeds and nuts and stir until all dry bits are coated and clumps have started to form.

2 ◆ Spread granola on a large rimmed baking sheet in a thin layer and bake 10–12 minutes. Remove from oven and gently move pieces from the edge to the center. Return to oven and bake an additional 10–12 minutes until golden brown. The granola will not be crunchy when it leaves the oven, but will crisp up as it cools. Once cool, transfer to an airtight container and store for up to 1 month.

❈❖❈ Blackberry Mint Smoothie

Serve this refreshing smoothie in the late summer when blackberries are at their peak. ⒟ **Serves 4**

*2 cups fresh or thawed frozen
    blackberries*
*1 cup plain yogurt (whole or
    low-fat)*

1/2 cup milk
3 tablespoons sugar
*2 tablespoons mint leaves,
    roughly chopped*

◆ Combine all ingredients in a blender and mix on high until smooth.

Peanut Butter and Banana Smoothie

This smoothie whirs together protein-packed peanut butter and nutrient-rich bananas for a sweet and wholesome breakfast treat. **D** **P** **Serves 2**

1/2 cup milk (or soy or almond milk)
2 bananas
1/4 cup natural peanut butter (smooth or chunky)

2 tablespoons maple syrup or honey
6 ice cubes

◆ Combine all ingredients in a blender and mix on high until smooth.

Greek Yogurt and Berry Parfait

Sweet, crunchy, creamy and filled with fresh fruit, this parfait delivers on every level. For a twist, try substituting labneh (a strained, Middle Eastern yogurt) for the Greek yogurt. **D** **Serves 2**

1 cup Greek yogurt (or regular yogurt, whole or low-fat)
1/2 cup fresh blueberries or blackberries
1/2 cup granola, store-bought or homemade (recipe page 47)

6 fresh strawberries, hulled and sliced
1 banana, sliced
2 tablespoons honey
2 tablespoons crystallized ginger, chopped (optional)

⟩TIP **IN A RUSH?**
Simply add yogurt to a bowl and top with other ingredients—the presentation might not be as special, but it will still taste great.

◆ Spread 1/4 cup yogurt into the bottom of a wide-rimmed glass. Top with 1/4 cup of blueberries or blackberries followed by 1/4 cup of granola. Add another layer of 1/4 cup yogurt followed by half of the banana slices and half of the sliced strawberries. Top with 1 tablespoon honey and 1 tablespoon crystallized ginger, if using. Repeat with second glass.

SALADS AND SPREADS

⊷◆⊶

“It is written, ‘He who makes the best egg salad shall rule over heaven and earth.’ Don't ask me why egg salad, I've got enough aggravation.” —WOODY ALLEN, *WHAT'S UP, TIGER LILY*, 1966

Salads and Spreads

No other food is quite as refreshingly elemental as a salad. Whether it is a simple pile of greens softened with olive oil and lemon juice or hearty Romaine hearts spiked with briny feta, a good salad embodies the bounty of the land at the sun-drenched height of summer.

◆ ◆ ◆

The Torah sets the stage for salad eating early on with God's declaration that “I have given you every herb yielding plant...and every tree [that bears fruit]—to you it shall be for food” (Genesis 1:29). And, over the centuries, human connection to these edible plants has manifested itself in countless delicious ways.

◆ ◆ ◆

The earliest proper salads likely date back to Roman times, when *herba salata* (Latin for “salted herbs”)—a dish of green vegetables tossed in salted water—graced dinner tables. In Jewish tradition, Ashkenazic cooks relied on pickled vegetables, particularly cucumbers, beets and cabbage, to infuse the cold winters of Eastern Europe with a bit of life and a necessary dose of nutrients.

Sephardic cuisine with its warm, Mediterranean influence is filled with small plates of mint- and parsley-flecked vegetable salads, salty olives and bean, eggplant and pepper-based spreads, which are served as a meze course. Contemporary Israeli food culture has vigorously adopted the meze tradition, vaulting *salatim* (Hebrew for "salads")—everything from hummus to the beloved chopped Israeli salad—into national icons.

◆ ◆ ◆

In America, the rise of sustainable agriculture, and particularly the growth of farmers' markets and Community Supported Agriculture programs, have made fresh, locally grown produce increasingly easy to find. They have also helped to introduce a myriad of less common vegetables to the American plate. Today, mesclun greens, arugula and watercress have joined iceberg lettuce at the salad bar. And whereas carrots and tomatoes were once the de facto mix-in options, salad lovers now enjoy an ever-growing palate of colors and flavors from which to create healthy, flavorful salad bowls.

◆ ◆ ◆

This chapter takes full advantage of that produce bounty by including dishes from across the salad spectrum. Vegetable-packed dishes like the **Asparagus Avocado Salad** *(page 56)* and **Panzanella Salad** *(page 57)* are joined by fruit-based ones such as the **Peach and Tomato Salad** *(page 65)* and **Moroccan Orange and Olive Salad** *(page 65)*, which deliciously blur the lines between sweet and savory. You will find light, *salatim*-style spreads like **White Bean Hummus with Frizzled Shallots** *(page 68)* and **Spicy Black Bean Dip** *(page 68)*, and salads that are substantial enough to serve as a meal, for instance the **Cucumber and Mint-Spiced Lamb Salad** *(page 58)*. Prefer to improvise? Check out the first featured "recipe," the **Mix-and-Match Salad Bar** that can inspire a new salad every night of the week.

PAGES 50–51: *Mix-and-Match Salad Bar, see box page 54*

Mix-and-Match Salad Bar

Avoid falling into a salad rut by consulting these salad bar ingredients. Select one or more items from each list—or add your personal favorites—and decide to go either dairy or meat when selecting proteins and cheeses. Then toss with dressing to enjoy a distinctly delicious salad for every day of the week. When making these salad bar-inspired dishes, exact quantities do not matter. Just follow the rule "two parts greens to one part mix-ins," and you will set yourself up for success. **D** **M** **P**

❧ GREENS

Arugula, Bibb lettuce, Boston lettuce, endive, escarole, mesclun greens, red leaf lettuce, romaine lettuce, spinach, watercress

❧ VEGETABLES AND FRUIT

Apple slices, artichoke hearts, avocado slices, baby corn, shredded or cooked beets, broccoli florets, shredded carrots, sliced celery, cherry tomatoes, corn kernels, sliced cucumber, grapefruit segments, halved grapes, sliced mushrooms, orange slices, pear slices, peas, diced pepper (red, yellow, green), pickles, shredded red cabbage, sliced red onion, snap peas, sliced strawberries, sprouts, sweet onion

❧ PROTEINS

Black beans, chickpeas, shredded chicken, sliced hardboiled egg, kidney beans, pinto beans, canned salmon, steak slices, tofu cubes, canned tuna, white beans

❧ CHEESES

Blue cheese, shredded cheddar cheese, feta cheese, goat cheese, shredded mozzarella cheese, shredded Parmesan cheese

❧ CRUNCHIES AND EXTRAS

Sliced almonds, black olives, green olives, croutons, hazelnuts, pecans, pistachios, raisins, walnuts, water chestnuts

A FEW PAIRING SUGGESTIONS:

❧ THE CLASSIC

Romaine + shredded carrots + cherry tomatoes + shredded chicken or tofu cubes + sliced almonds.
Suggested dressing: Lime Dressing (page 55)

❧ SAVORY AND TANGY

Mesclun + sliced cucumber + broccoli florets + chickpeas + artichoke hearts + feta + black olives.
Suggested dressing: Miso-Tahini Dressing (page 56)

❧ SWEET AND CRUNCHY:

Arugula + shredded beets + pear slices + halved grapes + goat cheese + pecans or walnuts.
Suggested dressing: Maple-Mustard Dressing (page 55)

❧ TART AND CREAMY

Escarole + avocado slices + white beans + grapefruit segments + shredded Parmesan.
Suggested dressing: Shallot dressing (page 55)

❧ STIR-FRY SALAD

Spinach + snap peas + sliced mushrooms + broccoli florets + steak slices + water chestnuts.
Suggested dressing: Lime Dressing (page 55)

⚜◆⚜ Lime Dressing

This light, lime-infused dressing tastes great on crunchy, vegetable-packed salads. Ⓟ **Makes approximately 1 cup**

1 clove garlic, minced
1/4 cup lime juice
1/4 cup olive oil

1/2 cup light olive oil
Salt and freshly ground black
* pepper to taste*

◆ Add all ingredients to a sealable container with a tight-fitting lid. Cover and shake vigorously until well combined, about 30 seconds.

⚜◆⚜ Maple-Mustard Vinaigrette

This twist on classic honey mustard dressing adds a touch of sweetness to any salad. Ⓟ **Makes approximately 1 cup**

1/2 cup vegetable oil
1/4 cup maple syrup
1/4 cup cider vinegar
2 tablespoons Dijon mustard
1 clove garlic, minced

2 tablespoons soy sauce
1/2 teaspoon salt
1/2 teaspoon freshly ground
* black pepper*

◆ Add all ingredients to a sealable container with a tight-fitting lid. Cover and shake vigorously until well combined, about 30 seconds.

⚜◆⚜ Shallot Dressing

This dressing tastes sophisticated but is simple to make. Ⓟ **Makes approximately 1/2 cup**

4 tablespoons olive oil
1 shallot, minced
1 clove garlic, minced
Juice of 1 lemon
1/2 cup finely chopped
* flat-leaf parsley*

1/2 teaspoon dried basil
1/2 teaspoon dried dill
1/2 teaspoon dried oregano
Salt and freshly ground black
* pepper to taste*

◆ Add all ingredients to a sealable container with a tight-fitting lid. Cover and shake vigorously until well combined, about 30 seconds.

✧◆✤ Miso-Tahini Dressing

This mix of smooth, nutty tahini and salty miso is a lovely dressing for salads and can also be drizzled onto sandwiches or grain dishes. ℗ **Makes approximately 1 cup**

3 tablespoons miso paste (any color)	1 teaspoon orange zest
3 tablespoons tahini	1 tablespoon chopped flat-leaf parsley
2 teaspoons lemon juice	1/4 cup water
2 tablespoons orange juice	1 teaspoon grated fresh ginger

◆ Add all ingredients to a blender and mix to combine, about 30 seconds.

✧◆✤ Asparagus Avocado Salad

Asparagus is one of the first vegetables ready for harvest after the long cold winter. Celebrate spring with this light and creamy salad. ℗ **Serves 4**

1 tablespoon white or red wine vinegar	Salt and freshly ground black pepper
Juice of half a lemon	1 1/2 pounds asparagus, ends trimmed off and sliced into 1/2-inch pieces
1/4 cup olive oil	2 medium ripe avocados
3 teaspoons sugar or honey	
1 tablespoon chopped fresh mint	
1 tablespoon chopped fresh cilantro	

1 ◆ In a medium bowl, whisk together the vinegar, lemon juice, oil, sugar, mint, cilantro and salt and pepper to taste; set aside.

2 ◆ Steam asparagus until just tender and still bright green, about 5 minutes. Remove from heat and plunge asparagus into cold water to stop cooking. Drain well and set aside.

3 ◆ Peel the avocados and slice the flesh into cubes. Put avocado and asparagus in a large bowl; drizzle with dressing and toss gently to coat.

⋈◆⋊ Panzanella Salad

This Tuscan bread-based salad turns a day-old loaf into a delicious summer treat. ⓟ **Serves 4–6**

1 French baguette (preferably a day old), cut into bite-sized cubes

8 plum tomatoes or 3 large heirloom tomatoes, seeded and chopped

2 kirby cucumbers (or 1 large seedless cucumber), chopped

1 small red onion, halved and thinly sliced

2 cloves garlic, minced

1/4 cup finely chopped basil

2 tablespoons finely chopped flat-leaf parsley

1/3 cup black olives, roughly chopped

1 15-ounce can white beans, rinsed and drained (optional)

3/4 cup olive oil

3 tablespoons red wine vinegar

2 tablespoons balsamic vinegar

Salt and freshly ground black pepper

1 ◆ Combine bread cubes, tomatoes, cucumbers, onion, garlic, basil, parsley, olives and beans, if using, in a medium bowl.

2 ◆ Whisk together oil, both vinegars and salt and pepper to taste in a small bowl. Drizzle over the salad and gently toss to coat bread. Allow to sit 15–30 minutes before serving.

⋈◆⋊ Israeli Caprese Salad

A healthy dash of dried za'atar lends Middle Eastern flavor to this Italian summer favorite. ⓓ **Serves 4**

1 medium-sized ball of mozzarella cheese

2 tomatoes

15 leaves fresh basil, washed and patted dried

1 tablespoon olive oil

1 1/2 teaspoons dried za'atar

Sea salt and freshly ground black pepper

◆ Slice the mozzarella and tomatoes into 1/4-inch rounds. Arrange the cheese, tomato slices and basil on a plate in an alternating pattern. Drizzle with olive oil, sprinkle with za'atar, then season with salt and pepper to taste.

❖◆❖ Cucumber and Mint-Spiced Lamb Salad

Prepare this filling dinner salad as an entrée for a quick and satisfying midweek meal. Ⓜ **Serves 4–6**

FOR SALAD:
2 tablespoons white wine vinegar
1 tablespoon olive oil
8 mint leaves, roughly chopped
Sea salt and freshly ground
*   black pepper*
1 English cucumber, julienned
2 carrots, julienned
4 scallions, thinly sliced
1/2 pound arugula

FOR LAMB:
1 teaspoon cumin
1 teaspoon chili powder
Sea salt and freshly ground
*   black pepper*
6 lamb chops
1 tablespoon olive oil

1 ◆ In a small bowl, whisk together vinegar, oil, mint leaves and salt and pepper to taste; set vinaigrette aside. Combine cucumber, carrots and scallions in a medium bowl and set aside.

2 ◆ *Make the lamb:* Preheat outdoor grill or grill pan over medium-high heat. Combine cumin, chili powder and salt and pepper to taste in a small bowl. Brush lamb chops with oil and season with spice mixture. Place lamb on preheated grill and sear on one side until browned, 3–4 minutes; flip and cook on second side another 3–4 minutes, until cooked through.

3 ◆ Spread arugula onto a serving platter and top evenly with cucumber-carrot mixture. Lay lamb chops on top of salad and drizzle with vinaigrette.

Cucumber and Mint-Spiced Lamb Salad ▶

✵✧✵ Roasted Butternut Squash Salad with Cranberries and Candied Pecans

Despite the added steps of roasting the squash and candying the pecans, this gorgeous sunset-colored salad comes together in about a half an hour. Pair it with a piece of baked tilapia (see **Tilapia Four Ways** page 150) or a quick spinach **Quasado** (page 161) for a scrumptious yet simple dinner. Store-bought candied pecans can be used to reduce preparation time. Ⓓ Ⓟ **Serves 4–6**

1 cup butternut squash, peeled,
seeded and cut into
1/2-inch cubes
5 tablespoons olive oil, divided
Sea salt
2 tablespoons butter or
non-hydrogenated margarine
2 tablespoons brown sugar

1/2 cup pecans
2 tablespoons red wine vinegar
2 teaspoons honey
Salt and freshly ground
black pepper
6 cups arugula or spinach
1/2 cup dried cranberries

1 ◆ Preheat oven to 400 degrees. In a bowl, combine squash cubes, 1 tablespoon oil and sea salt to taste, mixing thoroughly to coat squash with oil. Transfer squash to a rimmed baking sheet and roast for 20–25 minutes, until soft. Remove from oven and let cool.

2 ◆ Meanwhile, melt butter or margarine in a saucepan over medium heat. Once bubbling, stir in brown sugar, followed by pecans. Sauté pecans, stirring frequently, until coated with mixture, about 7 minutes. Remove from heat and allow to cool completely.

3 ◆ *Make the dressing:* Whisk vinegar, honey, 4 tablespoons oil and salt and pepper to taste in a small bowl.

4 ◆ *Assemble salad:* Combine arugula, squash, pecans and cranberries in a large bowl, drizzle dressing over and gently toss.

Roasted Butternut Squash Salad with ▶
Cranberries and Candied Pecans

❈◆❧ Honey Sesame Slaw

A drizzle of sesame oil and a splash of orange juice turn this cabbage slaw into something special. If you prefer, substitute 1/4 cup chopped toasted peanuts for the sesame seeds. Ⓟ Serves 6–8

1 1/2 teaspoons grated
   fresh ginger
1 1/2 tablespoons rice wine
   vinegar
2 tablespoons soy sauce
2 tablespoons orange juice
2 tablespoons honey
2 tablespoons vegetable oil
1 1/2 teaspoons sesame oil
1/2 teaspoon freshly ground
   black pepper

1 small head green cabbage,
   shredded
1 large carrot, peeled and
   grated
1/2 apple (like Fuji or Gala),
   unpeeled and grated
3/4 cup black raisins
1/4 cup toasted sesame seeds
3 scallions, thinly sliced

1 ◆ In a medium bowl, whisk together ginger, vinegar, soy sauce, orange juice, honey, vegetable oil, sesame oil and pepper; set aside.

2 ◆ Toss cabbage, carrot, apple and raisins together in a large bowl. Drizzle with dressing and toss again to coat. Top with sesame seeds and scallions.

❈◆❧ Late Summer Fig Salad

L uscious fresh figs pair perfectly with spicy watercress and creamy goat cheese in this end-of-summer treat. Ⓓ Serves 6

2 teaspoons honey
2 tablespoons lemon juice
4 tablespoons olive oil
2 bunches watercress, stems
   trimmed

24 ripe fresh figs, halved
   lengthwise
1/2 cup goat cheese, crumbled
Sea salt and freshly ground
   black pepper

1 ◆ Whisk honey, lemon juice and oil together in a medium bowl; set aside.

2 ◆ Spread watercress on a large serving platter and arrange figs on top. Scatter goat cheese around the figs, then drizzle with honey dressing. Finish with a sprinkle of salt and pepper to taste.

❧TIP *When fresh figs are out of season, substitute dried.*

◀ *Late Summer Fig Salad*

⋈◆⋊ Peach and Tomato Salad

Make this dish at the height of summer when juicy tomatoes and bright peaches are at their peak flavor and all over the farmers' market—and it's too hot to eat anything but salad anyway. **Ⓟ Serves 4–6**

2 teaspoons red wine vinegar	1 small red onion, quartered and
2 teaspoons sugar or honey	thinly sliced
2 tablespoons roughly	3 tomatoes
chopped fresh mint	3 ripe peaches, pitted
4 tablespoons olive oil	Salt and freshly ground black pepper

1 ◆ Whisk vinegar, sugar or honey, mint and oil together in a small bowl. Add the onion, stir to coat and let sit for 10 minutes to allow the flavors to mellow.

2 ◆ Meanwhile, slice the tomatoes and peaches into 1/4-inch wedges and add to a medium bowl. Add the onion mixture to the tomatoes and peaches and gently toss using a pair of tongs. Season with salt and pepper to taste.

⋈◆⋊ Moroccan Orange and Olive Salad

Claudia Roden writes in *The Book of Jewish Food* (Knopf) that orange and olive salads are a Moroccan specialty. If you can find them, red-fleshed blood oranges make an especially striking presentation. **Ⓟ Serves 4**

4 oranges (Valencia or blood	1/4 cup chopped flat-leaf parsley
oranges)	1 teaspoon paprika
1/4 cup oil-cured black olives,	1/2 teaspoon cumin (optional)
pitted and halved	3 tablespoons olive oil
2 tablespoons red wine vinegar	Sea salt and freshly ground
2 tablespoons honey	black pepper
1 clove garlic, minced	

1 ◆ Peel oranges, removing as much of the pith as possible, then slice horizontally into 1/4-inch rounds. Arrange orange slices on a serving platter and scatter with olives.

2 ◆ In a medium bowl, whisk together vinegar, honey, garlic, parsley, paprika, cumin (if using) and oil; drizzle over oranges and olives, then sprinkle sea salt and pepper to taste.

◀ *Moroccan Orange and Olive Salad*

❈◆❖ Radish Pickles

These refrigerator pickles make a zesty accompaniment to **Tuna Sandwich Niçoise** (page 78) and are a welcome addition to any meze platte. Ⓟ **Makes about 1 cup**

7 radishes, quartered
1 teaspoon salt
3 tablespoons rice vinegar
2 tablespoons sugar

1/2 teaspoon whole mustard seeds
1/2 teaspoon whole black peppercorns

1 ◆ Toss radishes with salt in a bowl and let stand 30 minutes. Drain in a sieve but do not rinse.

2 ◆ In a small saucepan, slowly heat vinegar and sugar over medium-low heat, stirring constantly, until sugar has completely dissolved, about 7 minutes. Remove from heat and add radishes, mustard seeds and peppercorns.

3 ◆ Transfer to a small bowl and let marinate in the refrigerator for at least 2 hours, or overnight.

⊰◆⊱ Eggplant and Red Pepper Salad

*C*reamy, charred eggplant makes a substantial and satisfying base for this lemony spread. Ⓟ **Serves 4-6**

2 medium eggplants
1/4 cup diced red bell pepper
1 clove garlic, chopped
1 scallion, sliced
2 tablespoons olive oil

2 tablespoons tahini
1/4 cup lemon juice
1/8 teaspoon cayenne powder
1/2 teaspoon salt

⇲TIP **BROILING EGGPLANT**

If you do not have a gas burner at home, you can broil the eggplants (turning them just as you would on the flame) until their skin is blistered and the inside is creamy and soft.

1 ◆ Turn stovetop gas burner to high and place eggplants, one at a time, directly over burner grate, turning occasionally with tongs until all sides are charred and eggplant is soft, about 5 minutes per side. Remove to a baking sheet and let cool completely. Drain juices, remove skin and place eggplant pulp in the bowl of a food processor.

2 ◆ Pulse eggplant 10–15 times until well chopped but with a few remaining chunks. Add red pepper, garlic, scallion, oil, tahini, lemon juice, cayenne and salt, pulsing to incorporate all ingredients. Transfer to a bowl, cover and refrigerate until serving.

⊰◆⊱ Guacamole with Chopped Egg

*J*ewish delicatessen tradition decrees that everything tastes better with a chopped egg—even guacamole! Ⓟ **Makes approximately 2 cups**

3 very ripe Haas avocados
Juice of 1 lime
1 clove garlic, minced
1/2 teaspoon kosher salt
1/2 medium red onion, diced

2 plum tomatoes, seeded and
   diced
2 hardboiled eggs, chopped
1 tablespoon chopped cilantro
   (optional)

1 ◆ In a large bowl, combine the avocado flesh, lime juice, garlic and salt, using a fork to mash the avocado.

2 ◆ Stir in the onion, tomatoes, hardboiled eggs and cilantro, if using. Let sit 10–15 minutes before serving.

❊✦❊ White Bean Hummus with Frizzled Shallots

This riff on chickpea hummus has a slightly mellower flavor than the original and tastes delicious spread on crackers, sandwiches or crostini. The frizzled shallots add an unexpected twist of sweet, caramelized flavor. ℗ **Serves 4–6**

FOR SHALLOTS:
Vegetable oil for frying
2 small shallots, thinly sliced
1/4 teaspoon salt

FOR HUMMUS:
1 large (19-ounce) can white beans (e.g. cannellini), rinsed and drained

2 tablespoons lemon juice
2 tablespoons tahini
1 clove garlic
1/2 teaspoon dried oregano
1/4 teaspoon salt
1/8 teaspoon freshly ground black pepper
1/3 cup olive oil, plus more for garnish

1 ◆ Fill a small, cold skillet with about 1/4-inch of vegetable oil. Add shallots and turn heat to medium-high. Cook until browned and crispy, 6–8 minutes.

2 ◆ Meanwhile, combine all hummus ingredients except oil in food processor; turn machine on and pour the oil into the mixture in a smooth stream. Process until smooth. Transfer hummus to a bowl and top with shallots and an additional drizzle of oil.

❊✦❊ Spicy Black Bean Dip

Fresh cilantro and cayenne add a satisfying zing to this hearty black bean spread. Layer it on sandwiches or use it as a dip for corn chips or pita. ℗ **Makes about 1 1/2 cups**

1 15-ounce can black beans, rinsed and drained
Juice of 1 lime
1/4 cup olive oil
2 cloves garlic

1/4 cup cilantro, roughly chopped
1/4 teaspoon salt
1/4 teaspoon cumin
1/4 teaspoon cayenne powder

◆ Put all ingredients into a blender or food processor and mix until smooth, stopping to scrape down the sides as needed. Store in an airtight container in the refrigerator.

Spicy Black Bean Dip and White ▶
Bean Hummus with Frizzled
Shallots, shown with Homemade
Pita Chips, recipe, page 204

⋈◆⋊ Walnut Pesto

Walnuts add deep, nutty flavor to this classic pesto. For a more traditional flavor, swap the walnuts with pine nuts. Set a bowl of pesto out as a dip for pita chips or stir it into cooked noodles for a quick and flavorful meal. Ⓓ **Makes about 1 1/2 cups**

2 cups packed basil leaves
1/3 cup walnuts, chopped
2 cloves garlic
1/2 cup olive oil

Juice of 1 lemon
1/2 cup Parmesan cheese
Salt and freshly ground black
  pepper

Pulse basil and walnuts in a food processor. Add garlic, oil and lemon juice and pulse again until smooth. Add Parmesan and salt and pepper to taste and pulse until just blended, pausing to scrape down the sides as needed. Will keep for up to a week stored in an airtight container in the refrigerator.

⋈◆⋊ Muhammara

This Middle Eastern red pepper-and-walnut spread is a tasty topping for baked fish, a dip for **Homemade Pita Chips** (page 204) or a spread for sandwiches. **Ⓟ Makes about 1 1/2 cups**

3/4 cup pomegranate juice
1/2 cup walnuts, toasted
1/4 teaspoon red pepper flakes
1/4 cup unseasoned breadcrumbs
2 tablespoons lemon juice
1 clove garlic (or more to taste)

1 16-ounce jar roasted red peppers, rinsed, drained and patted dry
1/2 teaspoon cumin
1 tablespoon olive oil
Salt

⇨TIP *If you can find pomegranate molasses, you can omit the step of reducing the juice and simply add 3 tablespoons of the molasses to the dish.*

1 ◆ Bring pomegranate juice to boil in a small saucepan set over high heat. Reduce heat to medium and cook, uncovered and stirring occasionally, until the juice is reduced to approximately 3 tablespoons, about 6 minutes. Set aside to cool.

2 ◆ Combine walnuts, red pepper flakes and breadcrumbs in a food processor and pulse until finely ground. Add the thickened pomegranate juice, lemon juice, garlic, red peppers, cumin and oil and pulse until smooth. Season with salt to taste. Transfer to a serving bowl, cover and refrigerate until serving.

SANDWICHES AND PIZZAS

Sandwiches and

If Jewish food culture can claim expert status on anything, the sandwich is certainly it. At the Passover Seder, Jews crunch into a Hillel sandwich—a curious mixture of bitter herbs and charoset on matza that recalls the paschal lamb "sandwich" eaten by Hillel the Elder in the 1st century B.C.E. While it hardly resembles the tuna fish on wheat or peanut butter and jelly we pack into our lunches today, Hillel's famous sandwich is often credited as the first.

◆ ◆ ◆

Fast-forward many centuries. The Jewish delicatessen introduced the world to the pastrami sandwich, an ethereal combination of sharp mustard and salty meat piled impossibly high on marbled rye. Delis are also responsible for adding corned beef, smoked brisket and egg salad

Pizzas

sandwiches to the American palate—the best things to happen to pickles since brine. And Israeli cuisine's love of a good sandwich (anything grilled or fried and stuffed into a pita) only deepens the Jewish-sandwich connection.

◆ ◆ ◆

With such a solid legacy gracing our collective heritage, it is only natural to devote an entire chapter of an everyday Jewish cookbook to the noble sandwich. As for the pizzas, just think of them as Italy's sandwich equivalent—alongside the panini—a portable, delicious and filling meal that is equally appropriate for lunch or dinner.

◆ ◆ ◆

While you won't find a pastrami recipe in this section (save those for the deli experts), you will find delicious flavor combinations, like a **Turkey Sandwich with Simple Fig-Onion Jam** *(page 77)*, quick **Veggie Wraps with Spicy Mayo** *(page 78)* and the vinaigrette-kissed **Tuna Sandwich Niçoise** *(page 78)*. On the pizza end, there are traditional red sauce varieties, such as **Artichoke, Pesto and Black Olive Pizza** *(page 87)* and **Sausage and Caramelized Onion Pizza** *(page 89)*, as well as more creative interpretations like **Fennel and Ricotta Pizza** *(page 90)*, which packs on tons of flavor without sauce. Any way you slice them, a satisfying, family-friendly meal is only about 20 minutes away.

PAGES **72–73**: *Artichoke, Pesto and Black Olive Pizza, recipe, page 87; Spinach, Peppers and Mozzarella Pizza, recipe, page 88; Fennel and Ricotta Pizza, recipe, page 90*

❧◆❧ Turkey Sandwich with Simple Fig-Onion Jam

Who says a turkey sandwich has to be boring? This fig-onion jam, ready in just 20 minutes, dresses up any sandwich. Mix things up by substituting chicken, sliced tofu or Brie in place of the turkey. **Ⓜ Makes 2 sandwiches**

2 tablespoons olive oil
1 onion, thinly sliced
2 tablespoons fig preserves
1 tablespoon balsamic vinegar
4 slices whole wheat or multigrain
 bread

6–8 ounces sliced cooked
 turkey breast
2 cups arugula
4 fresh figs, thinly sliced
 (optional)

1 ◆ Heat oil in a small saucepan over medium heat. Add onion and sauté, stirring occasionally, until browned, about 10 minutes. Add the fig preserves and balsamic vinegar; turn heat to low and cook, stirring frequently, until onions turn a deep brown, 5–10 more minutes. Remove pan from heat and let cool slightly.

2 ◆ Spoon fig-onion jam on two pieces of bread and layer turkey, arugula and fig slices, if using, on top. Top each sandwich with remaining pieces of bread. Slice in half before serving. Store any remaining jam in an airtight container in the refrigerator for up to two weeks.

❧◆❧ Hard-Boiled Sandwich

The mixture of hard-boiled egg, creamy avocado and tangy pickle slices in this sandwich will make you look forward to lunch. **Ⓟ Makes 4 sandwiches**

8 slices whole wheat bread
4 teaspoons mustard
4 teaspoons mayonnaise
 (optional)
4 hard-boiled eggs, sliced

1 avocado, sliced
1 dill pickle, thinly sliced
1 cup fresh spinach
Salt and freshly ground black
 pepper

1 ◆ Lay four slices of bread on a flat surface; spread 1 teaspoon mustard on each slice, followed by 1 teaspoon of mayonnaise, if using.

2 ◆ Top with egg slices, avocado, pickle, spinach and salt and pepper to taste. Cover with remaining four bread slices. If desired, slice in half.

◀ *Turkey Sandwich with Simple Fig-Onion Jam*

❈❖❈ Tuna Sandwich Niçoise

A crusty baguette makes the perfect package for this French-inspired sandwich. Ⓟ **Makes 4 sandwiches**

2 tablespoons red wine vinegar
3 tablespoons olive oil
1/2 teaspoon dried thyme
Salt and freshly ground black pepper
1 baguette, sliced into four pieces and halved
4 teaspoons Dijon mustard
2 5-ounce cans water-packed tuna

1/2 cup pitted Niçoise olives (or kalamata), sliced
4 pieces Bibb or Boston lettuce
1 medium cucumber, thinly sliced
1 small jar roasted red peppers
1/2 small red onion, thinly sliced

1 ◆ *Make the vinaigrette:* In a small bowl, whisk together the vinegar, oil, thyme and salt and pepper to taste; set aside.

2 ◆ *Assemble the sandwiches:* Spread 1 teaspoon mustard onto the bottom half of each baguette, then fill with tuna, olives, 1 piece of lettuce, cucumber slices, red pepper and red onion slices. Drizzle with vinaigrette just before serving

❈❖❈ Veggie Wraps with Spicy Mayo

Serve these delicious meat-free wraps for a quick and filling weeknight supper. If you have any of the bean mixture leftover, use it as an alternate topping to the **Broccoli Black Bean Nachos** (page 204). Ⓟ **Makes 4 wraps**

FOR THE WRAPS:
2 tablespoons olive oil
2 onions, halved and thinly sliced
1/2 teaspoon salt
1/4 teaspoon garlic powder
1/2 teaspoon dried oregano
2 15-ounce cans black beans, rinsed and drained
1 cup canned diced tomatoes, with liquid

4 flour tortillas or lavash bread
1 cup fresh spinach
2 avocados, sliced

FOR THE MAYONNAISE:
1/2 cup mayonnaise (light or regular)
2 teaspoons chili powder
2 tablespoons lime juice

1. ◆ Heat oil in large pan or cast-iron skillet over medium heat. Add onions and salt and cook, stirring occasionally, until browned, about 12 minutes. Add garlic powder, oregano, black beans and diced tomatoes with liquid and simmer until thick, 3–5 minutes.

2. ◆ *Make the spicy mayo:* Stir mayonnaise, chili powder and lime juice together in a small bowl until combined. (Store extra mayo in an airtight container in the refrigerator for up to 2 weeks.)

3. ◆ *Assemble the wraps:* Spread a layer of spicy mayo onto each tortilla; top with bean mixture, spinach and avocado. Roll and serve.

✕◆✕ Souped-Up Grilled Cheese

Souped-Up Grilled Cheese, photo page 107

There is nothing wrong with a simple grilled cheese sandwich, but a grilled cheese with fixings improves upon perfection. The trick to achieving a uniformly melted inside is to use grated cheese, which melts faster and more evenly than sliced cheese. Eat this sandwich alongside a steaming bowl of **Tuscan Tomato Soup** (page 106) for the ultimate grown-up comfort meal. Ⓓ **Makes 2 sandwiches**

4 slices multigrain bread
4 tablespoons unsalted butter, slightly softened
1/2–1 cup sharp cheddar cheese, shredded

Optional fixings: pesto, tomato slices, marmalade, apple slices, arugula, spinach, watercress, finely chopped sage leaves, **Simple Fig-Onion Jam** *(recipe page 77), avocado slices*

1. ◆ Heat a large nonstick pan over medium heat. Spread 1 tablespoon butter onto one side of each of the 4 bread slices. Place 2 of the slices on a flat surface, buttered-sides down. Add 1/4–1/2 cup cheddar to the 2 slices, followed by optional fixings. Top sandwiches with remaining slices of bread, buttered sides up.

2. ◆ Cook in heated pan until cheddar is melted and outside is lightly browned, 4–6 minutes per side.

✳✦✤ Hummus Sandwich Two Ways

While hummus sandwiches tend to be more virtuous than tasty, these two versions bring big flavor to the humble chickpea. Ⓓ Ⓟ **Makes 2 sandwiches**

BASIC SANDWICH:
4 slices multigrain bread

1/2 cup hummus

- Lay 2 slices of bread on a flat surface; spread 1/4 cup of hummus onto each slice. Add desired filling mixture (see below), then top with the other slices of bread.

BALSAMIC BEETS AND SPINACH: 1/2 cup fresh spinach + 1 small beet grated and tossed with 1 tablespoon balsamic vinegar and 1/2 teaspoon honey + 2 ounces crumbled feta cheese (optional)

TOMATO, CHEESE AND HONEY MUSTARD: 1 kirby cucumber thinly sliced + 4–6 slices of sharp cheddar cheese + 2 teaspoons honey mustard

✳✦✤ Goat Cheese Quesadilla

These Mexican-inspired "sandwiches" make a filling lunch or a great appetizer if you are hosting friends for a casual dinner. Throw in some black beans or pinto beans and serve with a salad for a no-fuss vegetarian weeknight dinner. Ⓓ **Makes 4 quesadillas**

4 flour tortillas
2 cups white cheddar or jack
*   cheese, grated*
8 ounces goat cheese, crumbled

1 cup packed arugula
Freshly ground black pepper
Topping ideas: salsa, avocado
*   slices*

1 ◆ Lay tortillas on a flat surface. Spread each with 1/2 cup cheddar, 2 ounces goat cheese and 1/4 cup arugula; sprinkle with pepper to taste.

2 ◆ Heat a large nonstick pan over medium heat. Brush lightly with vegetable oil or lightly coat with cooking spray. Fold the tortillas in half, taking care that the fillings remain inside. Place two of the folded tortillas in the pan and cook until cheese is melted and outsides are lightly browned, 3–5 minutes per side.

3 ◆ Place finished quesadillas on a baking sheet in a 200-degree oven to keep warm while cooking the remaining two. Finish with desired toppings and cut into wedges.

Goat Cheese Quesadilla ▶

❊◆❊ Sabich

Here is a simple rendition of an Iraqi Jewish classic popular throughout Israel. **Ⓟ Makes 2 sandwiches**

1 medium eggplant, sliced into
   1/4-inch rounds
Salt
Vegetable oil for frying
2 medium tomatoes, seeded and
   chopped
1/4 cup chopped flat-leaf parsley

2 kirby cucumbers, seeded
   and chopped
1/2 small red onion, chopped
4 very fresh whole pitas
3/4 cup hummus
4 hard-boiled eggs, sliced
1/4–1/2 cup tahini
Hot sauce

1 ◆ Generously sprinkle eggplant slices with salt, place on a baking sheet and let sit for 20–30 minutes. Press eggplant slices between two clean dishtowels (or paper towels) to remove excess moisture.

2 ◆ Heat 1 inch of oil in a large frying pan over medium-high heat. Working in batches, fry eggplant until it is dark brown, about 5 minutes on the first side and 3 minutes on the second side. Remove from oil and drain on paper towels.

3 ◆ In a medium bowl, combine the tomatoes, parsley, cucumbers and onion. Slice pita pockets open; spread a few tablespoons of hummus inside each, then fill with egg slices and eggplant slices and about 1/2 cup of the tomato mixture. Drizzle with tahini and hot sauce to taste.

Sabich ▶

✂◆✂ Carrot, Black Bean and Feta Pita

Grated carrots and creamy black beans make a wholesome and delicious filling for pita. The filling can also be eaten alone as a tasty bean salad. Ⓓ **Makes 2 sandwiches**

2 medium carrots, peeled and
   grated
1 15-ounce can black beans,
   rinsed and drained
Juice of half a lemon
1/2 teaspoon sugar or honey
1/2 teaspoon cumin
1 tablespoon olive oil

1/4 cup mint, finely chopped
Salt and freshly ground
   black pepper
2 very fresh whole pitas
4 pieces romaine lettuce or
   1/2 cup salad greens
4–8 ounces feta cheese,
   crumbled

⇢TIP *Change up this sandwich by substituting pinto or kidney beans for the black beans.*

1 ◆ In a medium bowl, combine the carrots, black beans, lemon juice, sugar or honey, cumin, oil, mint and salt and pepper to taste; stir well.

2 ◆ Slice pita pockets in half, then stuff each pocket with lettuce followed by 1/4 of the carrot and black bean mixture and top with 1–2 ounces crumbled feta.

◀ *Carrot, Black Bean and Feta Pita*

�〜◆〜 Basic Pizza Dough

Waiting around for dough to rise is not necessarily an everyday pursuit, but when you have the time, give it a try—it's worth the wait. ℗ **Makes 2 balls of dough**

1 package dry yeast
1 1/4 cups warm water (should be hot, but not scalding)
1 teaspoon sugar
3 cups all-purpose flour

1/2 cup whole wheat flour*
1 tablespoon salt
2 tablespoons plus 1 teaspoon olive oil, divided

1 ◦ In a small bowl, combine yeast, water and sugar and let sit until yeast is dissolved, about 5 minutes.

2 ◦ In a large bowl, combine both flours and salt; make a well in the flour and set aside.

3 ◦ Whisk 2 tablespoons oil into yeast mixture, then pour mixture into the flour well. Stir with a wooden spoon to combine, then gather dough together and transfer to a lightly floured surface. Knead until smooth and pliable, 5–10 minutes. (If dough is too sticky, add small amounts of flour while kneading.)

4 ◦ Coat flour bowl with 1 teaspoon oil; transfer dough to bowl, flip once to coat with oil then cover with a clean dishtowel or plastic wrap and allow to rise in a warm place (like your stove top) until doubled in size, 1 to 1 1/2 hours.

5 ◦ Punch dough down and divide in half. Pat each piece into a ball and let rest, loosely wrapped in a towel or plastic wrap, for at least 10–15 minutes. Roll out and add desired toppings. If only using one ball, wrap the second tightly in plastic wrap and store in the freezer for up to 6 months. Thaw completely before rolling out.

*Experiment with using more or less whole wheat flour until you find a ratio you like.

BUYING PIZZA DOUGH
◆ ◆ ◆ ◆ ◆

Good quality pizza dough is increasingly easy to find at supermarkets and health food stores. At the market, look for it in either the refrigerated or frozen foods sections, and read ingredients carefully to avoid brands that load their dough with unnecessary preservatives or ingredients. Most pizza shops will also happily sell you a ball or two of their freshly made dough to use in your kitchen.

❖◆❖ Basic Pizza Sauce

Store-bought pizza sauce is a blessing when you are short on time, but nothing beats the taste or smell of homemade sauce simmering on the stove. Try it when you have the time and embellish it—with sliced bell peppers, mushrooms, olives, etc.—any way you like. **Ⓟ Makes about 2 cups**

2 tablespoons olive oil
1 medium onion, finely chopped
2 cloves garlic, minced
1/2 teaspoon dried basil
1/2 teaspoon dried oregano

1 28-ounce can diced tomatoes,
  with liquid
1 tablespoon tomato paste
Salt and freshly ground black
  pepper

1 ◆ Heat the oil in a medium saucepan over medium heat. Add the onion and cook, stirring occasionally, until browned, 8–10 minutes. Stir in garlic, basil and oregano and cook for another 2 minutes until fragrant.

2 ◆ Add the diced tomatoes with liquid and tomato paste, lower heat slightly and let simmer until thickened, 20–25 minutes. Season with salt and pepper to taste.

❖◆❖ Artichoke, Pesto and Black Olive Pizza

Tangy artichoke hearts and olives mingle with zesty pesto on this super-quick pizza. **Ⓓ Serves 4**

1/4 cup cornmeal
1 ball pizza dough
1 cup pizza sauce
1/2 cup mozzarella cheese, grated
1/4–1/2 cup pesto
  (e.g., Walnut Pesto, page 70)

1/2 cup water-packed artichoke
  hearts, quartered
1/2 cup black olives, pitted and
  sliced
1/2 teaspoon dried basil

1 ◆ Preheat oven to 450 degrees. Scatter cornmeal evenly over a large baking sheet. Stretch or roll dough into a 10–12-inch round and place on sheet.

2 ◆ Spread pizza sauce over the dough, followed by mozzarella. Dollop teaspoonfuls of pesto around pizza, then top with artichoke hearts, olives and a sprinkle of basil. Bake for 15–17 minutes, until crust is puffed and crispy and cheese is slightly browned.

Artichoke, Pesto and Black Olive Pizza, photo page 72

Sauteed Kale and Goat Cheese Pizza

Soft, earthy kale pairs perfectly with mild goat cheese, toasted pine nuts and lemon zest on this pizza. Dress a salad of greens with a drizzle of olive oil and a squeeze of the lemon you zested and dinner is served. Ⓓ **Serves 4**

2 tablespoons olive oil
1 onion, chopped
1 bunch kale, stemmed and chopped
Sea salt and freshly ground black pepper
1/4 cup cornmeal

1 ball pizza dough
1 cup pizza sauce
1/2 cup pine nuts, toasted
1/2 cup mozzarella cheese, grated
1 5-ounce container goat cheese
Zest of 1 lemon

1 ◆ Heat oil in a large pan over medium heat. Add onions and cook, stirring occasionally, until onions soften and begin to caramelize, about 6 minutes. Add kale to the skillet and season with salt and pepper to taste. Add 1 teaspoon of water, cover skillet and cook until kale wilts, 5–6 more minutes.

2 ◆ Meanwhile, preheat oven to 450 degrees. Scatter cornmeal evenly over a large baking sheet. Stretch or roll dough into a 10–12-inch round and place on sheet. Spoon sauce over dough and top with onion and kale mixture, pine nuts, mozzarella, goat cheese and lemon zest. Bake for 15–17 minutes, until crust is puffed and crispy and cheese is slightly browned.

MICROPLANE ZESTER
◆ ◆ ◆ ◆ ◆

Buying a microplane grater is a worthwhile investment. They yield fluffy, fragrant citrus zest that practically melts into recipes and also make short work of grating Parmesan cheese, fresh nutmeg and many other kitchen tasks. In a pinch, however, the small perforations on a standard box grater produce a slightly coarser, but entirely usable, zest.

Spinach, Peppers and Mozzarella Pizza

This simple, satisfying topping combination is a true classic. Ⓓ **Serves 4**

1 tablespoon olive oil
1 cup red bell pepper, seeded and sliced
1/2 teaspoon garlic powder
Salt and freshly ground black pepper
2 cups fresh spinach

1/4 cup cornmeal
1 ball pizza dough
1 cup pizza sauce
1–1 1/2 cups mozzarella cheese, grated
1/2 teaspoon dried thyme

Spinach, Peppers and Mozzarella Pizza, photo page 73

1 ◆ Heat oil in a large pan over medium heat. Add peppers and cook, stirring occasionally, until soft, 6–7 minutes. Add garlic powder, salt and pepper to taste and stir. Next, add spinach and cook, stirring occasionally, until wilted but still bright green, about 3 minutes.

2 ◆ Meanwhile, preheat oven to 450 degrees. Scatter cornmeal evenly over a large baking sheet. Stretch or roll dough into a 10–12-inch round and place on sheet. Spoon sauce over dough, followed by mozzarella; top with peppers and spinach mixture. Sprinkle thyme over top and bake 15–17 minutes, until crust is puffed and crispy and cheese is slightly browned.

⋈◆⋈ Sausage and Caramelized Onion Pizza

Piled with sweet caramelized onions and dotted with spicy sausage, this pizza tastes great even without the cheese. Ⓜ **Serves 4**

2 tablespoons olive oil
2 sweet onions (e.g., Vidalia or Walla Walla), halved and thinly sliced
Salt
1/4 cup cornmeal
1 ball pizza dough

1 1/4 cups pizza sauce
1/2 teaspoon dried rosemary
1/2 teaspoon dried thyme
2 links kosher sausage (or veggie sausage), sliced into 1/4-inch pieces

1 ◆ Heat oil in a large pan over medium heat. Add onions and salt to taste and cook, stirring occasionally, until deep brown and caramelized, 12–15 minutes.

2 ◆ Preheat oven to 450 degrees. Scatter cornmeal evenly over a large baking sheet. Stretch or roll dough into a 10–12-inch round and place on sheet. Spread pizza sauce over the dough, then sprinkle with rosemary and thyme. Top with onion mixture and sausage. Bake for 12–15 minutes, until crust is puffed and crispy.

❖◆❖ Fennel and Ricotta Pizza

Sweet fennel and creamy lemon-spiked ricotta make an unusual—and delicious—white pizza pairing. Ⓓ **Serves 4**

1 tablespoon olive oil
1 fennel bulb, thinly sliced
Sea salt
1 cup ricotta cheese (whole fat or skim)
1 teaspoon lemon zest
1/4 cup cornmeal

1 ball pizza dough
1/2 cup arugula
1/4 teaspoon dried tarragon
1/4 cup Parmesan cheese, grated
Salt and freshly ground black pepper

▼ *Fennel and Ricotta Pizza*

1 ◆ Heat oil in a large pan over medium heat. Add fennel and a sprinkle of sea salt and let cook, stirring occasionally, until softened, about 5 minutes. Meanwhile, in a small bowl stir together the ricotta and lemon zest.

2 ◆ Preheat oven to 425 degrees. Scatter cornmeal evenly over a large baking sheet. Stretch or roll dough into a 10–12-inch round and place on sheet. Spread ricotta over the dough and top with arugula and the sautéed fennel. Sprinkle on tarragon and Parmesan, followed by additional salt and pepper to taste. Bake for 15–17 minutes, until crust is puffed and crispy and Parmesan is slightly browned.

⊰◆⊱ Za'atar Pitza

In a pinch you can always use pita as the base of a pizza, but in this classic Middle Eastern street food, pita is the intentional star of the show. **P** **Serves 4**

4 whole wheat pitas
4 tablespoons olive oil
4 tablespoons za'atar

3 plum tomatoes, sliced into
* rounds and deseeded*
Sea salt

1 ◆ Preheat oven to 375 degrees. Arrange pitas on a large baking sheet; drizzle each with 1 tablespoon oil and sprinkle with 1 tablespoon za'atar.

2 ◆ Arrange a few tomato slices on top of each pita and sprinkle with salt to taste. Bake until just crisp, 6–8 minutes.

SOUPS AND STEWS

Soups and Stews

Every year, right around the high holidays, the weather seems to suddenly click from summer to fall. August's intense heat, endless iced coffees and Sunday beach trips fade, making way for autumn's crisp air, vibrant treetops and knit scarves. And, of course, with the cool weather also comes an intensified craving for warm, nourishing bowls of soup.

◆ ◆ ◆

Not surprisingly, Jewish cuisine, which knows a thing or two about creating comfort through food, has made numerous contributions to the soup world—from matza ball soup and the iconic chicken soup with noodles, known affectionately as *goldene yoich* (golden broth) and "Jewish penicillin," to jewel-toned borscht, mushroom barley soup and mouth-puckering sorrel schav. These soups are the culinary embodiment of home—long-simmering affairs that fill the house with warmth and fragrance and graciously beckon you to the table.

Even if you do not have the time to fuss over a pot of boiling chicken bones (and that kind of time is rare these days), don't let your busy schedule lure you toward the canned soup aisle. While convenient, canned soups often come with serious sodium counts and other nutritional baggage. There are plenty of fresh soup options that deliver on comfort and taste without the hefty time commitment.

◆ ◆ ◆

This section includes jazzed-up classics like **Lemony Chicken Soup** *(page 96)* and **Tuscan Tomato Soup** *(page 106)*, which are at once surprising and soothingly familiar. You will find brothy soups like **Ginger Miso Soup with Brown Rice** *(page 98)* and the more substantial **Steak Stir-Fry Soup** *(page 96)* to curl up with, hearty stews such as **Mushroom Lentil Soup** *(page 108)* and **Drunken Vegetable Chili** *(page 111)*, and a **Caramelized Vegetable Soup** *(page 102)* that has all the silkiness of a creamy soup without the dairy. So when the weather cools down (or any time the soup craving strikes), think of this section as your edible equivalent of a cozy fall sweater.

PAGES 92–93: *Sweet Potato Kale Soup with White Beans, recipe, page 97*

❖❖ Lemony Chicken Soup

This is a traditional chicken noodle soup only brighter, thanks to the lemon juice and zest. Ⓜ **Serves 6–8**

1 cup spiral-shaped pasta
2 tablespoons olive oil
1 small onion, finely chopped
2 large cloves garlic, finely
    chopped
3 stalks celery, chopped
2 medium carrots, diced
8 cups chicken broth

2 cups shredded cooked chicken
Juice of 1 lemon
1 teaspoon lemon zest
2 tablespoons chopped dill
2 tablespoons chopped flat-leaf
    parsley
Salt and freshly ground black
    pepper

1 ◆ Cook pasta in a pot of salted water according to package directions, drain and set aside.

2 ◆ Heat oil in a large stockpot or Dutch oven over medium heat. Add onion and sauté until just translucent, 5–6 minutes. Add garlic, celery and carrots and sauté until vegetables are tender, about 8 minutes.

3 ◆ Add broth and bring soup to a boil, then reduce heat and simmer 20 minutes. Add chicken, lemon juice, lemon zest, dill and parsley and simmer an additional 5 minutes. Season with salt and pepper to taste. Divide pasta into bowls and ladle soup over pasta.

❖❖ Steak Stir-Fry Soup

There's no need for a wok with this soup—all the flavors of stir-fry are waiting in your bowl. Ⓜ **Serves 6–8**

2 tablespoons olive oil
1 pound skirt steak, trimmed
    of excess fat and cut into
    1/2-inch strips
1 onion, sliced
1 leek, thinly sliced
3 cloves garlic, minced
2 carrots, sliced
2 stalks celery, sliced
1 1/2 cups white button
    mushrooms, sliced

6 cups chicken broth
Red pepper flakes
Salt and freshly ground black
    pepper
2 tablespoons cornstarch
3 tablespoons water
1 cup fresh spinach, chopped
1 cup snow peas
1/2 cup bean sprouts
    (optional)

Leeks and scallions (also called green onions) add rich, piquant flavor to any dish. But with their similar-looking bulbous white heads and green stalks, some home cooks confuse them in the kitchen.

When using leeks (long and fat), wash them thoroughly to release any dirt stuck in their crevices. Pat dry and then slice just the white and light green parts of the leek. Discard the dark green tops. With scallions (long and skinny), wash and pat dry before slicing. Both the white and dark green parts of the scallion can be used.

1 ◆ Heat oil in a large stockpot or Dutch oven over medium heat. Add the steak, onion, leek, garlic, carrots, celery and mushrooms and sauté, stirring frequently, until the beef begins to brown and the vegetables are just tender, about 8 minutes.

2 ◆ Add the broth, red pepper flakes and salt and pepper to taste and bring to a boil.

3 ◆ In a small bowl, combine the cornstarch and water to make a paste and stir into soup.

4 ◆ Add the spinach and snow peas and allow soup to boil for an additional 3 minutes before serving. Garnish with bean sprouts, if using.

⚹◆⚹ Sweet Potato Kale Soup with White Beans

This nourishing soup gets its rich flavor from roasted garlic, luscious sweet potatoes and tender pieces of kale. If you like a brothier soup, increase the amount of broth to taste. Ⓟ Serves 6–8

1 head garlic
3 tablespoons olive oil, divided
2 leeks, thinly sliced
1 sprig fresh thyme
4 medium-sized sweet potatoes, peeled and cut into 1/2-inch pieces
6 cups vegetable or pareve chicken broth

1 small bunch kale, stems removed, chopped
1 14-ounce can white beans (e.g. cannellini), rinsed and drained
1 teaspoon salt
1/2 teaspoon freshly ground black pepper

1 ◆ Preheat oven to 400 degrees. Slice top off the garlic head, exposing the tops of the cloves. Drizzle with 1 tablespoon oil, wrap lightly with aluminum foil and bake for 30 minutes. Remove from the oven and let cool. Squeeze the cloves out of their shells into a small bowl and set aside.

2 ◆ While garlic is roasting, heat remaining oil in a large stockpot or Dutch oven over medium heat. Sauté the leeks and thyme sprig until leeks become translucent, about 8 minutes. Add sweet potatoes and continue cooking, stirring frequently, until potatoes begin to soften, 10 minutes.

3 ◆ Add roasted garlic and broth; bring to a low boil, cooking until potatoes are tender, about 12 minutes. Add kale and white beans and cook just until kale begins to wilt, about 4 minutes. Remove thyme sprig, season with salt and pepper and serve immediately.

Sweet Potato Kale Soup with White Beans, photo pages 92–93

❧◆❧ Greens and Orzo Soup

Silky orzo and tender greens make a lovely pair in this vitamin-packed soup. **Ⓓ Ⓟ Serves 4–6**

1/2 cup orzo
2 tablespoons olive oil
1 medium onion, chopped
3 cloves garlic, minced
4 cups vegetable or pareve
    chicken broth
2 cups water
1 cup snow peas

1 small (or 1/2 medium) bunch of
    greens (kale, collards, Swiss chard,
    etc.), stems removed, chopped
Salt and freshly ground black
    pepper
Juice of half a lemon
1/4 cup shredded Parmesan
    cheese (optional)

1 ◆ Cook orzo according to package directions (leave it slightly al dente because it will continue to cook once added to soup). Rinse with cold water, drain and set aside.

2 ◆ Heat oil in a large stockpot or Dutch oven over medium heat. Add the onion and garlic and sauté until translucent, 7–8 minutes. Add the broth and the water, bring to a boil, then reduce heat, add snow peas and simmer until they are slightly soft, 4–5 minutes.

3 ◆ Add the greens and salt and pepper to taste and simmer until greens are just wilted, about 3 minutes. Turn off heat, stir in cooked orzo and lemon juice and ladle soup into bowls. Serve topped with shredded Parmesan, if desired.

❧◆❧ Ginger Miso Soup with Brown Rice

Miso soup is Japan's equivalent to chicken soup—fragrant, nourishing and good for whatever ails you. **Ⓟ Serves 4–6**

3/4 cup short-grain brown rice
1 tablespoon olive oil
1 small onion, cut into
    half-moons and thinly sliced
2 cloves garlic, minced
1 teaspoon grated fresh ginger
6 cups water

1/3 cup crimini or white button
    mushrooms, thinly sliced
1/2 package extra-firm tofu, cut
    into 1/4-inch cubes
1/4 cup brown or red miso paste
    (or more to taste)
1 cup packed fresh spinach leaves
3 scallions, thinly sliced

1 ◆ Cook rice according to package instructions; set aside.

2 ◆ Heat oil in a large stockpot or Dutch oven over medium heat. Add onion, garlic and ginger and sauté, stirring occasionally, until lightly browned, 6–8 minutes.

3 ◆ Add water (scraping up any browned bits with a wooden spoon), mushrooms and tofu, bring to a simmer and cook about 15 minutes. Remove pot from heat.

4 ◆ In a small bowl, dissolve miso paste with 1/2 cup of the warm broth and then stir it into the pot along with spinach and scallions. Divide the rice into bowls and ladle soup over.

⋈◆⋈ Classic Minestrone

Do not let the long ingredient list deter you from trying this delicious, quick-simmering specialty. Ⓓ Ⓟ **Serves 6**

3 tablespoons olive oil	*1 28-ounce can crushed or diced tomatoes*
1 large sweet onion (e.g. Walla Walla or Vidalia), diced	*4 cups vegetable broth*
6 cloves garlic, minced	*1 cup water*
2 stalks celery, diced	*Salt and freshly ground black pepper*
1 large carrot, diced	*1 can white beans (e.g., cannellini)*
2 small zucchinis, diced	*1/4 cup chopped flat-leaf parsley*
1 bay leaf	*Parmesan cheese for garnish (optional)*
1 tablespoon chopped fresh thyme (or 1 teaspoon dried)	
1 tablespoon chopped fresh oregano (or 1 teaspoon dried)	

1 ◆ Heat oil in a large stockpot or Dutch oven over medium heat. Add onions and sauté until translucent, about 7 minutes. Add garlic, celery, carrot and zucchinis and sauté until vegetables start to soften, about 10 minutes. Add bay leaf, thyme and oregano and sauté for 1 additional minute, until fragrant.

2 ◆ Stir in tomatoes, broth and water; bring to a simmer and cook until vegetables are tender, about 20 minutes.

3 ◆ Season soup with salt and pepper to taste. Add beans and parsley and turn off heat. Ladle into bowls and garnish with Parmesan, if desired.

STORE-BOUGHT BROTH

● ● ● ● ●

The supermarket carries many varieties of pre-made broths—flavorful, fragrant liquids made by simmering water with meat or vegetables—to use as a quick base for soups. The two broths used most frequently in this book are vegetable broth and pareve chicken broth, which echoes the flavor of traditional chicken broth without the meat. At the store, always look for low-sodium broths (you can adjust the salt according to taste in the cooking process), and stay away from any broth that contains monosodium glutamate (MSG).

❈◆❈ Supa de Fasole Verde

This Romanian Jewish green bean soup is adapted from a dish in the cookbook *Ca la Mama Acasa: Bucate Traditionale Evreiesti* (Hasefer). Pickle fans will especially love its briny punch and dill-infused flavor. The chickpeas are an addition to the original recipe, but add heft to an otherwise all-vegetable soup. **D** **P** **Serves 4–6**

3 tablespoons vegetable oil or
    olive oil
6 large cloves garlic, sliced
2 tablespoons all-purpose flour
1 teaspoon paprika
6 cups water
4 1/2 cups fresh or thawed
    frozen green beans, cut into
    1/2 inch pieces
2 large tomatoes, chopped
    (with seeds and juice)

1 1/2 tablespoons red or white
    wine vinegar
2 tablespoons sugar
Sea salt and freshly ground black
    pepper
1/4 teaspoon red pepper flakes
1/4 cup chopped flat-leaf parsley
1/4 cup chopped dill
1 15-ounce can chickpeas, rinsed
    and drained (optional)
Sour cream for garnish (optional)

1 ◆ Heat oil in a stockpot or Dutch oven over medium heat. Add garlic and fry until just browned, 3–4 minutes. Add flour and paprika and stir to coat garlic.

2 ◆ Add water to the pot and bring to a boil; lower heat, add green beans, tomatoes and vinegar and simmer until green beans are soft, 10–12 minutes (if using thawed frozen green beans, simmer for 8–9 minutes).

3 ◆ Stir in sugar, salt and pepper to taste, red pepper flakes, parsley, dill and chickpeas (if using) and cook an additional 2 minutes. Serve hot with a dollop of sour cream, if desired.

HERBS AND SPICES: FRESH VS. DRIED

● ● ● ● ●

Using fresh herbs is a wonderful way to boost the flavor of any dish, but there's no need to ditch most recipes just because you do not have fresh herbs on hand. In general, you can substitute 1 teaspoon of dried herbs for 1 tablespoon of fresh herbs. Add dried herbs near the beginning of the cooking process to allow them to open up; add fresh herbs at the end so they keep their flavor.

A similar logic applies to spices. Buying whole dried spices and grinding them at home (in a spice grinder or with an immersion blender) delivers the most potent flavors. But if you only have preground spices on hand—such as nutmeg—go ahead and substitute them at a 1:1 ratio.

Supa de Fasole Verde ▶

❈❖❈ Quick(er) Borscht

Borscht is known for its long simmering time and rich beet flavor. This version delivers on the taste while cutting the cooking time in half. This soup tastes better the second—and even the third—day, so make a pot on Sunday and enjoy it well into the week. **D** **P** **Serves 8–10**

3 large beets, peeled	*1 teaspoon allspice*
2 carrots, peeled	*1/2 cup tomato paste*
1/2 small head of cabbage	*8 cups pareve chicken or beef broth*
1 large onion	*2 bay leaves*
1/4 cup olive oil	*Salt and freshly ground black pepper*
8 cloves garlic, chopped	*Sour cream for garnish (optional)*

1 ◆ In a food processor fit with the shredding attachment, shred beets, carrots, cabbage and onion. (You can also grate the vegetables by hand using the largest holes on a standard box grater.)

2 ◆ Heat the oil in a large stockpot or Dutch oven over medium heat; sauté shredded vegetables and garlic, stirring occasionally, until they are just tender, 8–10 minutes. Add allspice and tomato paste and cook for additional 1 minute.

3 ◆ Add broth and bay leaves; bring to a boil then reduce heat and simmer, stirring occasionally, until vegetables are soft, 30–35 minutes. Remove bay leaves, season with salt and pepper to taste and serve with a dollop of sour cream, if desired.

❈❖❈ Caramelized Vegetable Soup

This flavor-packed, dairy-free soup gets its creamy texture from the whir of an immersion blender. **P** **Serves 8**

6 tablespoons vegetable oil	*6 cups water*
2 onions, chopped	*1 1/2 teaspoons salt*
2 medium leeks, thinly sliced	*Salt and freshly ground*
4 cloves garlic, chopped	*black pepper*
2 stalks celery, chopped	*Chopped flat-leaf parsley for*
2 carrots, chopped	*garnish (optional)*
1 teaspoon dried thyme	*Herbed croutons for garnish*
1 large potato, peeled and cut	*(optional)*
into 1/2-inch pieces	

1 ◆ Heat oil in a large stockpot or Dutch oven over medium-high heat. Add onions, leeks, garlic, celery and carrots and sauté, stirring occasionally, until vegetables are browned, 15–17 minutes. Stir in thyme and cook for 1 additional minute, until fragrant.

2 ◆ Add potatoes, water and salt; bring to a boil and then reduce heat. Cover partially and simmer until potatoes are tender, about 12 minutes. Turn off heat and let cool for a minute.

3 ◆ Using an immersion blender or a standard blender working in batches, purée the soup until smooth. (If using standard blender, return creamed soup to the pot.) Season with additional salt and pepper to taste, ladle into bowls and garnish with parsley and croutons, if desired.

⊁◆⊱ Creamy Soups Four Ways

This recipe is versatile enough to carry you through all four seasons and basic enough to let the flavors of seasonal produce shine through. ⓓ **Serves 4**

1 tablespoon olive oil
1/2 cup chopped onion
1 1/2 cups pareve chicken broth
2 tablespoons butter or margarine
2 tablespoons all-purpose flour

1/4 teaspoon salt
Salt and freshly ground black
  pepper
1 cup milk

1 ◆ Heat oil in a large stockpot or Dutch oven over medium heat. Add onion and sauté, stirring occasionally, until just translucent, about 6 minutes. Add broth and vegetables-and-seasoning mixture (see below); bring to a boil, then reduce heat to simmer, partially cover and allow vegetables to cook until tender. Turn off heat.

2 ◆ Using an immersion blender or a standard blender working in batches, purée the soup until creamy. (If using standard blender, return creamed soup to the stockpot.)

3 ◆ In a pan, melt butter or margarine over medium-low heat. Add flour and stir constantly until a thick roux forms, about 3 minutes. Add milk, salt and pepper to taste and cook, stirring constantly, until thick, about 7 minutes. Whisk milk mixture into vegetable purée and serve warm. If desired, thin soup by adding more broth.

⊰ WINTER SOUP
SWEET POTATO AND CARROT: 1 cup sweet potato, peeled and cut into 1/2-inch cubes; 1/2 cup carrots, peeled and cut into 1/2-inch circles; 1 tablespoon brown sugar; 1 teaspoon cinnamon; 1/2 teaspoon ground ginger; a pinch of nutmeg. Soup simmering time: 15–20 minutes.

⊰ SPRING SOUP
SPINACH AND SWEET PEA: 1 cup packed baby spinach leaves; 1/2 cup fresh or thawed frozen sweet peas; 2 tablespoons chopped fresh mint. Soup simmering time: 5–7 minutes. Serve hot or cold.

⊰ SUMMER SOUP
CORN AND TOMATO: 3/4 cup fresh or thawed frozen corn kernels; 1/2 cup plum tomatoes, seeded and roughly chopped; 1/2 teaspoon dried tarragon. Soup simmering time: about 10 minutes.

⊰ FALL SOUP
POTATO LEEK: 1 large leek, sliced and sautéed in 1 tablespoon butter or margarine (use in place of the oil and onion); 1 1/2 cups potato, peeled and cut into 1/2-inch cubes; 1 teaspoon dried thyme. Soup simmering time: 15–20 minutes.

◀ *Creamy Soup: Spinach and Sweet Pea*

❊◆❊ Tuscan Tomato Soup

This sumptuous, herb-filled take on classic tomato soup pairs perfectly with a **Souped-Up Grilled Cheese** sandwich (page 79). Ⓓ Ⓟ **Serves 6**

1 cup olive oil
4 cloves garlic, roughly chopped
1 French baguette or loaf of Italian bread, crusts removed and torn into small pieces
1 28-ounce can whole peeled tomatoes (with juice and seeds)
4 cups vegetable broth (or water)

1 teaspoon chopped fresh rosemary (or 1/3 teaspoon dried rosemary)
5–6 basil leaves, torn into small pieces
Kosher salt and freshly ground black pepper
Croutons for garnish (optional)
Parmesan cheese for garnish (optional)

⇒TIP *If desired, purée with an immersion blender or in a standard blender in batches before serving. For a more rustic look, leave unblended.*

1 ◆ Heat oil in a large stockpot or Dutch oven over medium-low heat. Add garlic and sauté until just fragrant, about 3 minutes. Add bread and sauté, stirring constantly, until all the oil is absorbed and the bread is toasted, about 7 minutes.

2 ◆ Pour tomatoes into a medium bowl and, using your hands, squeeze the tomatoes until broken into small pieces.

3 ◆ Add tomatoes, broth, rosemary, basil and salt and pepper to taste to pot with bread; bring to a boil, then reduce heat. Simmer until the bread breaks down, about 20 minutes. Top with croutons and grated Parmesan, if serving with a dairy meal.

Tuscan Tomato Soup shown ▶ *with Souped-Up Grilled Cheese, recipe page 79*

❊❖❊ Mushroom Lentil Soup

Creamy cooked lentils and fragrant spices combine in this hearty soup—the perfect antidote to a cold, dreary day. Ⓓ Ⓟ **Serves 4–6**

2 tablespoons olive oil
1 onion, chopped
1/2 cup crimini mushrooms, chopped
1 cup chopped carrots
4 cloves garlic, chopped
1 1/2 teaspoons cumin
1 1/2 teaspoons coriander
1/2 teaspoon chili powder

2 cups French or green lentils
8 cups vegetable broth
Juice of 1 lemon
1 teaspoon salt
1/2 teaspoon freshly ground black pepper
Chopped flat-leaf parsley for garnish (optional)
Plain yogurt (optional)

1 ◆ Heat oil in a large stockpot or Dutch oven over medium heat. Add the onion and sauté, stirring occasionally, until soft and translucent, about 8 minutes.

2 ◆ Add mushrooms, carrots and garlic and cook until just softened, another 7 minutes. Add the cumin, coriander and chili powder and cook for additional 1 minute, stirring constantly, until spices are fragrant.

3 ◆ Add the lentils and broth and simmer 35–40 minutes until lentils are soft and creamy. Stir in the lemon juice, salt and pepper, adjusting seasoning to taste. Serve topped with chopped parsley and yogurt, if desired.

⚓◆⚓ Simple Pea Soup with Leeks

Seriously short on time? Try this super fast, super satisfying spring-inspired soup. Ⓜ Ⓟ **Serves 4–6**

2 tablespoons olive oil	4 cups vegetable or chicken broth
1 large leek, thinly sliced	1 1/2 cups fresh or thawed frozen
1/2 teaspoon salt	green peas
1 teaspoon dried dill, plus more	Salt and freshly ground black
for sprinkling	pepper

1 ◆ In a large stockpot or Dutch oven, heat oil over medium heat. Add leeks and salt and sauté, stirring occasionally, until leeks are soft and lightly browned, 8–10 minutes. Add dill and let cook for additional 1 minute until fragrant.

2 ◆ Add broth and peas and cook over medium-low heat until warmed through, 7–10 minutes. Remove from heat and season with additional salt and pepper to taste.

3 ◆ Using an immersion blender or a standard blender working in batches, pureé the soup until smooth. Divide into bowls and sprinkle with additional dill, if desired.

SEITAN
⋆⋆⋆⋆⋆

Despite its funny name, seitan (pronounced SAY-TAN) is a delicious, soy-free meat alternative. It is derived from wheat flour mixed with water and sometimes referred to as "wheat meat." If you have ever eaten mock chicken, duck or beef at a vegetarian Chinese restaurant, your dish was most likely made from seitan.

Seitan is readily available in health food stores and becoming more common in supermarkets. It often comes packed in tubs but can also be found preseasoned and cut into ready-to-cook strips.

⚓◆⚓ Seitan and Tomato Stew

Served over steamed white rice or **Caramelized Onion Rice** (page 132), this saucy vegetarian stew makes a hearty weeknight meal. Ⓟ **Serves 4**

2 tablespoons olive oil	1/4 cup dry red wine
1 onion, diced	1 8-ounce package seitan, cut
1 teaspoon dried oregano	into bite-sized pieces
1 teaspoon dried basil	1 28-ounce can diced tomatoes
1/2 teaspoon dried rosemary	1/2 cup pitted kalamata olives
1/2 teaspoon dried thyme	(or any type), roughly
1/2 teaspoon garlic powder	chopped

1 ◆ Heat oil in a large sauté pan or cast-iron skillet over medium heat. Add onion and cook, stirring occasionally, until browned, about 8 minutes. Add oregano, basil, rosemary, thyme and garlic powder and cook another minute until the mixture becomes very fragrant. Deglaze pan with the wine, scraping up any browned bits, and cook for 2–3 minutes.

2 ◆ Add seitan and tomatoes and let mixture simmer for 15–20 minutes. Just before serving, turn off heat and stir in olives.

✥◆✥ Drunken Vegetable Chili

Red wine adds saucy depth to this quick-simmering vegetarian chili. Serve in a bowl over rice, topped with shredded cheese and scallions. Ⓓ Ⓟ **Serves 4–6**

2 tablespoons olive oil
1 large onion, chopped
1 large red pepper, seeded and
    chopped
1 jalapeño pepper, seeded and
    chopped
3 cloves garlic, chopped
1 tablespoon cumin
2 tablespoons chili powder

1/2 cup dry red wine
1/2 cup vegetable broth
1 32-ounce can crushed tomatoes
1 15-ounce can black beans, rinsed
    and drained
1 15-ounce can kidney beans,
    rinsed and drained
1 cup ground soy vegetable
    crumbles (optional)

1 ◆ Heat oil in a large stockpot or Dutch oven over medium heat. Add onion, red pepper, jalapeño and garlic and sauté 5–7 minutes until softened. Stir in the cumin and chili powder and cook for 2 minutes, until fragrant. Deglaze the pan with the wine, scraping up any browned bits, and simmer for another 2–3 minutes.

2 ◆ Add the broth, tomatoes, black beans, kidney beans and vegetable crumbles, if using, and stir to combine. Simmer over low heat for 15–20 minutes until slightly thickened.

◀ *Drunken Vegetable Chili*

SIDES

·····◦◆◦·····

Sides

Sherlock and Watson. Lucy and Ricky. Batman and Robin. In each of these iconic duos, the sidekick played an integral role in defining the team. They had personality and spunk and were often scene-stealing stars as well as supporting actors. When it comes to dinner, side dishes should take notes from their pop culture counterparts.

❖ ❖ ❖

In American cooking, side dishes have too often been marginalized to the edge of our plates, and for good reason. The bland mounds of rice, starchy potatoes and overcooked vegetables that commonly pass for sides offer little in the way of taste-bud excitement. In contrast, a truly delicious side dish is far more than filler and certainly more than an afterthought. A side dish should complement and elevate a meal, helping to highlight the main course while solidly holding its own at the table.

The recipes in this section restore rightful dignity to the humble side dish. There are flavorful vegetables like **Garlicky Sautéed Greens** *(page 116)* and **Ginger Sesame Green Beans** *(page 117)*—both simply prepared to allow the produce to shine. You will find potato dishes like **Grilled Herbed Potatoes** *(page 122)* and grain-based sides like **Warm Barley, Apple and Feta Salad** *(page 132)* and **Couscous with Dried Cherries and Mint** *(page 135)* that run flavor circles around plain old white rice.

❖ ❖ ❖

Picnics and backyard barbecues will benefit from updated Jewish classics like **Grilled Tzimmes** *(page 125)* and crowd pleasers from **Basil Two-Bean Salad** *(page 136)* to **Lemony Spaghetti Pasta Salad** *(page 136)*. And some of the sides, like **Polenta with Tomatoes, Shallots and Goat Cheese** *(page 128)*, are so hearty you might just decide to skip the entrée altogether. On a *kashrut* note, while several of the sides in this section include a sprinkling (or more!) of cheese, in most cases the dairy can be easily removed when serving the dish alongside a meat meal.

PAGES **112–113:** *Thyme-Roasted Root Vegetables, recipe, page 123*

REMOVING STEMS FROM GREENS

· · · · ·

Kale, collard greens, Swiss chard and other leafy greens often come with tough, woody stems. To remove them, fold the leaf in half along the stem line. With one hand grasping the stem right where it meets the leaf, use the other hand to rip away the leaf from the stem. Set aside de-stemmed leaves while finishing the rest and discard or compost the stems.

❖❖❖ Garlicky Sautéed Greens

A bit of garlic and a dash of tamari are all it takes to bring out the best in leafy greens. **D** **P** Serves 4

2 tablespoons olive oil
2 bunches greens (kale, collards, Swiss chard, etc.), stems removed, chopped
2 cloves garlic, thinly sliced

2 teaspoons tamari or soy sauce
1 teaspoon lemon juice (optional)
1/4 cup grated Parmesan cheese (optional)

1 ◆ Heat oil in a large pan over medium heat. Rinse chopped greens thoroughly, drain and add to pan along with garlic, stirring gently to coat with oil (there should still be a little water clinging to the leaves). Cover and cook until greens are soft and wilted, 6–8 minutes.

2 ◆ Uncover and add tamari and lemon juice, if desired, stirring to coat. Re-cover and cook an additional 1–2 minutes. Serve topped with grated Parmesan, if desired.

Lemony Asparagus

Fresh springtime asparagus needs few embellishments. Here, a drizzle of lemon and olive oil add a burst of bright flavor. **P** Serves 4–6

3 tablespoons olive oil	2 bunches asparagus,
Juice of 1 lemon	bottoms trimmed off
2 cloves garlic, minced	Sea salt and freshly ground
	black pepper

1 • Preheat oven to 425 degrees. In a small bowl, whisk together oil, lemon juice and garlic.

2 • Arrange the asparagus spears in a single layer on a baking sheet or roasting pan. Drizzle with oil and lemon mixture and roll to evenly coat each spear.

3 • Roast in the oven until just tender, about 10 minutes.

TAMARI VS. SOY SAUCE

• • • • •

Soy sauce and tamari are both dark, savory condiments made from fermented soybeans. They are largely interchangeable in cooking, though Japanese tamari tends to be richer in flavor and less salty than its Chinese counterpart. Some tamari brands are also wheat free, which makes them compatible for people with gluten sensitivities.

Ginger Sesame Green Beans, photo page 156

Ginger Sesame Green Beans

Serve these sweet and savory green beans alongside **Maple Glazed Chicken Teriyaki** (page 142) or **Pan Fried Tofu with Peanut Sauce** (page 155). If desired, substitute fresh broccoli florets for the green beans. **P** Serves 4

1 pound green beans, ends	1 tablespoon minced garlic
snapped off	1 teaspoon grated fresh ginger
1 tablespoon olive oil	1 teaspoon sesame oil
Kosher salt	1/4 teaspoon red pepper flakes
1 tablespoon tamari or soy sauce	Freshly ground black pepper
2 tablespoons honey	Toasted sesame seeds (for garnish)

1 • Preheat oven to 425 degrees. Spread beans in a 9 x 13-inch baking dish; drizzle with oil and sprinkle with salt to taste. Toss to coat beans evenly with oil and salt and roast for 10 minutes.

2 • Meanwhile, combine tamari or soy sauce, honey, garlic, ginger, sesame oil and red pepper flakes in a small bowl.

3 • Remove beans from oven. Pour tamari-sesame mixture over beans and toss to coat evenly. Return beans to oven and roast for 10–12 additional minutes, until browned and starting to shrivel. Transfer to serving plate and sprinkle with additional salt, black pepper and sesame seeds to taste.

✧◆✧ Sweet Corn with Lime and Chili Butter

Serve this street food favorite at home and enjoy the best flavors of summer. Ⓓ Ⓟ **Serves 4–6**

6 ears fresh sweet corn, shucked	*1 teaspoon lime juice*
1/2 cup unsalted butter or non-hydrogenated margarine, softened	*1/2 teaspoon chili powder*
	1/2 teaspoon salt

1 ◆ Bring a large pot of salted water to a boil. Add corn and cook until just softened, about 6 minutes; drain.

2 ◆ Meanwhile, combine butter or margarine, lime juice, chili powder and salt in a small bowl and stir until completely incorporated.

3 ◆ Serve butter alongside corn or slather approximately 1 teaspoon onto each ear of corn before serving. Reserve any leftover butter in an airtight container in the refrigerator.

✧◆✧ Pan-Roasted Brussels Sprouts with Toasted Almonds

Forget the waterlogged, boiled Brussels sprouts you avoided as a kid: These caramelized beauties are destined to be a new favorite. Ⓟ **Serves 4–6**

2 tablespoons olive oil	*1 teaspoon water*
3/4 pound Brussels sprouts, washed and quartered	*2 teaspoons tamari or soy sauce*
2 cloves garlic, minced	*1/2 cup slivered almonds*

1 ◆ Heat oil in a large pan over medium heat. Add Brussels sprouts, garlic and 1 teaspoon water; cover with a tight-fitting lid and cook, stirring occasionally, until Brussels sprouts are soft and browned, about 8 minutes. Stir in tamari or soy sauce, re-cover and cook for an additional 2 minutes.

2 ◆ While sprouts are cooking, heat small pan over medium heat; add almonds and toast, stirring occasionally, until browned and fragrant, about 7 minutes. Sprinkle over Brussels sprouts just before serving.

Pan-Roasted Brussels Sprouts ▶
with Toasted Almonds

❧❧ Honey-Glazed Carrots with Za'atar

The hint of earthy za'atar in this dish offers a welcoming counter-point to the sweetness of the honey. Ⓟ **Serves 4–6**

1/4 cup olive oil
3 tablespoons za'atar, divided
1/2 teaspoon salt
6 carrots (about 2 1/2 pounds),
    cut into 1/4-inch coins

3 tablespoons honey
1/2 teaspoon lemon zest
Freshly ground black pepper

1 ◆ Preheat oven to 400 degrees. Combine oil, 2 tablespoons za'atar and salt in a bowl. Add carrots and toss to combine.

2 ◆ Spread carrots in one layer in a large baking dish, drizzle with honey and roast for 40 minutes, stirring once, until carrots are slightly wilted and charred. Remove from oven, cool slightly and sprinkle with honey, remaining za'atar, lemon zest and pepper and additional salt to taste.

BRAISING
◆ ◆ ◆ ◆ ◆

Braising is a French cooking technique that combines wet and dry heat to bring out food's flavor. Most braising follows the same basic process of first searing the meat or vegetables over high heat, then slowly simmering them with a bit of liquid until softened and fork-tender.

❧❧ Braised Fennel

Serve this tender fennel side alongside **Miso Ginger Chicken** (page 145). Ⓜ Ⓟ **Serves 4**

2 large or 3 small fennel bulbs,
    stems and fronds removed
3 tablespoons olive oil
1 small onion, diced
3 stalks celery, diced
1 large carrot, diced

2/3 cup white wine
2/3 cup chicken or vegetable
    broth
Juice of half a lemon
Salt and freshly ground black
    pepper

1 ◆ Halve fennel bulbs; remove core with two diagonal cuts in a V toward the center. Then quarter the bulbs.

2 ◆ In a large pan with a lid, heat oil over medium heat. Add onion, celery and carrot and cook until browned and softened, 5–6 minutes. Add fennel pieces and cook for an additional 6 minutes, until fennel starts to brown.

3 ◆ Add white wine, broth and lemon juice, lower heat and cover the pan. Simmer until fennel is soft all the way through, 15–20 minutes.

Red Winter Braise

Cabbage is a winter staple at farmers' markets. Braising—cooking in liquid—makes the cabbage tender and delicious. It tastes even better the next day, once the flavors have had time to meld.

M P **Serves 8**

1 tablespoon olive oil
1 medium red onion, thinly sliced
2 cloves garlic, thinly sliced
2 cups chicken or vegetable broth
1 1/2 cups dry red wine
1 cup packed brown sugar

1/2 cup plus 2 tablespoons
  balsamic vinegar
1 head red cabbage (about
  3 pounds), cut into
  1-inch pieces
1 large apple, cored and grated

1 ◆ Preheat oven to 350 degrees. Heat oil in an oven-safe, deep sauté pan or a stockpot over medium-high heat. Add onion and cook, stirring until soft and translucent, 5 minutes. Add garlic and cook 1 additional minute. Add broth, wine, brown sugar and vinegar and stir to dissolve sugar. Add cabbage and apple, stir to combine, raise heat to high and bring to a boil.

2 ◆ Reduce heat and simmer for 10 minutes. Cover and transfer to oven; braise for 45 minutes, until cabbage is tender.

3 ◆ Remove cabbage from oven and stir in remaining 2 tablespoons vinegar. Serve warm or at room temperature.

❊❖❊ Grated Beets with Toasted Hazelnuts

Grating beets significantly reduces their cooking time, which means getting dinner on the table faster. **Ⓓ Ⓟ Serves 4**

1 tablespoon olive oil
2 medium beets, grated
1/2 cup chopped hazelnuts
1 tablespoon lemon juice or red wine vinegar

1/4 cup chopped flat-leaf parsley
Salt and freshly ground black pepper
3 ounces goat cheese, crumbled (optional)

1 ◆ Heat oil in a large pan over medium heat. Add beets and sauté until slightly softened, 5–7 minutes.

2 ◆ Meanwhile, add hazelnuts to a small pan over medium-low heat and toast, stirring occasionally, until browned and fragrant, about 7 minutes.

3 ◆ Stir lemon juice and parsley into beets and cook 2 additional minutes. Remove from heat; season with salt and pepper to taste and add goat cheese, if using. Sprinkle hazelnuts on top before serving.

❊❖❊ Grilled Herbed Potatoes

These soft, lightly charred potatoes make the perfect side dish for any summer barbecue. Try serving them alongside **Cumin and Cilantro Burgers** (page 158) or **Portobello Burgers** (page 160). **Ⓟ Serves 4–6**

1 1/2 pounds Yukon Gold potatoes, cut into 1/2-inch slices
1/4 cup olive oil
2 tablespoons lemon juice
2 tablespoons chopped flat-leaf parsley, plus more for sprinkling

2 cloves garlic, minced
Salt and freshly ground black pepper
1/2 teaspoon paprika

1 ◆ Put potatoes in a large pot filled with salted, boiling water. Cook for 6 minutes until slightly tender but not fully cooked; drain well.

2 ◆ In a large bowl, whisk together oil, lemon juice, parsley, garlic and salt and pepper to taste. Add cooked potatoes to bowl and toss gently to coat.

❊TIP **PERFECT POTATOES**

Before grilling, make sure potatoes are drained thoroughly. Get rid of any excess water by returning the cooked, drained potatoes to the pot, turning the burner to low heat and letting them cook for 1-3 minutes until moisture has evaporated.

3 ◆ Heat outdoor grill or grill pan to medium-high heat. Put potatoes on grill and cook until tender and slightly charred, flipping once, about 8 minutes total. Transfer potatoes to a plate, drizzle with any remaining marinade, sprinkle with additional chopped parsley and season with paprika and additional salt and pepper to taste.

❖◆❖ Thyme-Roasted Root Vegetables

The trick with this dish is to cut everything to the same size so it all cooks evenly. You can swap rosemary for the thyme, mix and match vegetables (try parsnips, other varieties of squash, Brussels sprouts, etc.) or stick with one type of vegetable (for instance, all potatoes). ⒹⓅ **Serves 4**

▼ Thyme-Roasted Root Vegetables

*2 medium beets, peeled and cut into
    1/2-inch pieces*
*2 Yukon gold, red bliss or blue potatoes,
    peeled and cut into 1/2-inch pieces*
*2 medium sweet potatoes, peeled and
    cut into 1/2-inch pieces*
*1 Delicata squash, unpeeled, cut into
    1/2-inch slices*
*2 medium carrots, cut into 1/2-inch
    pieces*
2 tablespoons olive oil
2 teaspoons dried thyme
1 teaspoon salt

1 ◆ Preheat oven to 400 degrees. Combine beets, potatoes, sweet potatoes, squash and carrots in a large bowl. Add oil, thyme and salt and toss to coat vegetables.

2 ◆ Spread vegetables onto a large, rimmed baking sheet and bake for 25 minutes. Open oven and move vegetables around with a wooden spoon, then bake for an additional 25–30 minutes until vegetables are soft and browned.

Grilled Tzimmes

Re-create the flavors of this Rosh Hashana mainstay on your backyard grill. ⓟ **Serves 4**

2 sweet potatoes, peeled and cut into 1/4-inch rounds
2 carrots, halved vertically and cut into 1-inch pieces
3 apricots, halved and pitted
2 red pears, cored and quartered

4 tablespoons olive oil, divided
2 tablespoons brown sugar
1 teaspoon cider vinegar
Salt and freshly ground black pepper
3 tablespoons raisins (optional)

1 ◆ Preheat grill or grill pan to medium heat. In a large bowl, toss sweet potatoes, carrots, apricots and pears with 2 tablespoons oil and salt and pepper to taste.

2 ◆ Grill vegetables and fruit in batches, starting with the sweet potatoes and carrots (about 8 minutes, covered and turning once), followed by the apricots and pears (4-5 minutes, turning once). Arrange grilled vegetables and fruits on a platter.

3 ◆ Whisk together brown sugar, cider vinegar, remaining 2 tablespoons oil and salt and pepper to taste in a small bowl. Drizzle dressing over the vegetables and sprinkle with raisins, if using.

Sweet Potato Fries

These oven-baked fries are a lighter version of a comfort-food favorite, so dig in and enjoy! ⓟ **Serves 4–6**

2 large sweet potatoes, peeled and cut into 1/4-inch thick strips

3–4 tablespoons olive oil
Sea salt and freshly ground black pepper

1 ◆ Preheat oven to 425 degrees. In a large bowl, toss sweet potatoes with enough oil to coat well and salt and pepper to taste. Transfer potatoes to a large rimmed baking sheet, making sure they do not overlap and that the baking sheet is not overcrowded (use two if necessary).

2 ◆ Bake for 15 minutes, then flip potatoes (tongs work well for this) and bake for another 7–10 minutes until browned and crispy. Sprinkle with additional salt and pepper to taste.

VARIATIONS: Add 1/2 teaspoon dried spice or ground herb (thyme, rosemary, cumin, coriander or some combination) to the mix.

◀ *Grilled Tzimmes*

❧◆❧ Baked Onion Rings

This diner-classic remake proves to be as delicious as the deep-fried original. **Ⓓ Serves 4**

2 cups breadcrumbs (ideally
    Panko)
1/2 teaspoon cayenne powder
1 teaspoon dried thyme
2 large eggs
1/2 cup low-fat buttermilk
1/4 cup all-purpose flour

Salt and freshly ground black
    pepper
4 tablespoons olive oil
1 large sweet onion (e.g. Vidalia
    or Walla Walla), sliced
    into 1/4-inch rounds and
    separated into rings.

1 ◆ Preheat oven to 450 degrees. In a medium bowl, mix bread-crumbs, cayenne and thyme; set aside. In another medium bowl, whisk together eggs, buttermilk, flour and salt and pepper to taste.

2 ◆ Dip onion rings into egg mixture, then dredge in herbed bread-crumbs; place on a large plate and set aside.

3 ◆ Pour oil onto a rimmed baking sheet and place in the oven for 2 minutes. Carefully remove sheet from oven and tilt to spread oil around. Place onion rings on sheet in one layer, making sure they do not overlap. Bake for 8 minutes, then turn rings over and bake an additional 8 minutes until rings are crispy and golden brown. Sprinkle with additional salt to taste.

❧◆❧ Pickle-Kissed Potato Salad

This salad is the perfect quick summer side for a barbecue with friends or family. **Ⓟ Serves 6**

1/2 cup chopped red onion
2 tablespoons pickle juice
1 1/2 pounds red potatoes, peeled
    and cut into 1/2-inch pieces
2 hard-boiled eggs, roughly
    chopped

1/2 cup diced celery
1/4 cup chopped flat-leaf parsley
1/2 cup mayonnaise
1/4 cup chopped kosher dill
    pickles
Freshly ground black pepper

1 ◆ Place onion and pickle juice in a small bowl and let sit for at least 10 minutes to allow the onion to mellow.

2 ◆ Boil potatoes in a large pot filled with salted water and cook until tender, about 10 minutes. Drain well and set aside to cool slightly.

3 ◆ Combine onion mixture, cooked potatoes, eggs, celery, parsley, mayonnaise, pickles and pepper to taste in a large bowl. Mix gently until ingredients are blended. If desired, add additional mayonnaise to taste. Serve at room temperature or cover and refrigerate.

⊰◆⊱ Colcannon

This take on the classic Irish dish of cabbage mashed potatoes makes exceptionally good use of autumn farmers' market produce.
D P Serves 6–8

3 pounds russet potatoes, peeled and cut into 1-inch pieces (about 5 cups)
1 teaspoon salt, divided
4 cups kale, stems removed and chopped
1/4 cup finely chopped chives

1 1/3 cups milk or almond milk
4 tablespoons butter or non-hydrogenated margarine
1/2 teaspoon garlic powder
1/4 teaspoon freshly ground black pepper

1 ◆ Place potatoes and 1/2 teaspoon salt in a large saucepan; cover potatoes with cold water. Bring to a boil and cook 5 minutes. Add kale and boil 3 more minutes, until potatoes are tender and kale is wilted; drain.

2 ◆ Meanwhile, put chives, milk, butter or margarine, remaining 1/2 teaspoon salt, garlic powder and pepper in a medium saucepan; bring to a boil, then immediately remove from heat.

3 ◆ Return drained potatoes and kale to large saucepan and coarsely mash. Gradually add milk and chive mixture, continuing to mash and stir until light and fluffy.

Polenta with Tomatoes, Shallots and Goat Cheese

This savory side doubles as a quick one-dish entrée for vegetarians. The finished product looks especially pretty with multicolored cherry tomatoes, like the ones you will find at the farmers' market in summer. ⓓ **Serves 4**

1 tablespoon olive oil
2 shallots, chopped
1 cup cherry tomatoes, halved
1/2 teaspoon dried thyme
1/2 teaspoon dried basil

2 cups water
1 cup milk
1/2 teaspoon salt
1 cup polenta or yellow cornmeal
1 tablespoon unsalted butter
1/4 cup goat cheese, crumbled
Freshly ground black pepper
*1/4 cup grated Parmesan cheese
(optional)*

1 ◦ In a small saucepan, heat oil over medium heat. Add shallots and sauté, stirring occasionally, until translucent, about 3 minutes. Add tomatoes and cook until they begin to soften, another 4 minutes. Add thyme and basil and sauté for another minute, then remove from heat.

2 ◦ In a medium pot, combine water, milk and salt and cook over medium heat until simmering (but not quite boiling). Pour in polenta in a steady stream while stirring vigorously with a wooden spoon. Bring mixture to a boil, then reduce heat and allow polenta to simmer, stirring constantly, until mixture turns creamy and thick, about 7 minutes.

3 ◦ Turn off heat; add butter and stir to incorporate. Gently fold in the tomato-shallot mixture, goat cheese and pepper and additional salt to taste. Serve sprinkled with Parmesan, if desired.

Quinoa Mango Salad with Lime-Cumin Dressing

Quinoa is lauded for its high protein content, but rarely noted for its flavor. With its mix of sweet mango and spicy cumin dressing, this side offers the best of both worlds. **(P) Serves 4–6**

FOR SALAD:
1 cup quinoa
2 mangoes, peeled and diced
1 bunch watercress, stems
    removed and roughly chopped
    (or 2 cups packed fresh
    spinach leaves)

FOR VINAIGRETTE:
1/3 cup vegetable oil
Zest and juice of 1 lime
2 teaspoons cumin
2 teaspoons grated fresh ginger
2 teaspoons brown sugar
1/8 teaspoon cayenne powder
Salt and freshly ground black
    pepper

1 ◆ Cook quinoa according to package directions; remove from heat and set aside.

2 ◆ Whisk together oil, lime zest and juice, cumin, ginger, brown sugar, cayenne and salt and pepper to taste in a small bowl. (Or add to a jar with a tight-fitting lid and shake vigorously until combined, about 30 seconds.)

3 ◆ Add quinoa to a large bowl and toss with 1/2 of the vinaigrette. Add the mango and watercress and toss, adding just enough additional dressing to lightly coat. Tightly seal and refrigerate any leftover dressing.

DELICATA SQUASH

Delicata squash—sometimes called Bohemian squash—is a delicious winter squash that is quickly joining its more popular cousins such as butternut and acorn squash at the farmers' market and supermarket. The Delicata is oblong-shaped, ranging from 5–10 inches in length. The skin, which is light yellow with vertical green lines, is edible when cooked, and the flesh is creamy and slightly sweet, almost like a chestnut.

❧◆❧ Quinoa-Stuffed Squash with Pears and Cranberries

The quinoa in this dish makes it a hearty and nourishing vegetarian entrée as well as a delicious autumnal side. Everything comes together while the squash roasts—then it's just stuff and serve. **(P) Serves 10**

6 Delicata squashes, halved
 length-wise, seeds removed
 (or substitute 5 small acorn
 squashes)
5 tablespoons olive oil, divided
2 cups vegetable broth
1 cup quinoa
2 firm Bosc or red pears, chopped
1 small red onion, diced

1 stalk celery, diced
1 sprig fresh thyme, leaves
 removed from stalk (or
 1 teaspoon dried thyme)
1/3 cup dried cranberries
1/3 cup pecans, chopped
Salt and freshly ground black
 pepper
2 tablespoons honey (optional)

1 ◆ Preheat oven to 425 degrees. Line a baking sheet with parchment paper or foil. Rub squash flesh with 3 tablespoons oil and place face up on the baking sheet. Roast for 25–30 minutes until flesh is easily pierced with a knife. (If using acorn squash, roast for 30–35 minutes.) Remove from oven and cool.

2 ◆ Meanwhile, in a saucepan bring broth to a boil; stir in quinoa, lower heat and simmer, covered, according to package directions. When quinoa is done cooking, turn off the heat, add diced pears and cover the pot to allow pears to steam for a few minutes.

3 ◆ In a medium pan, heat remaining 2 tablespoons oil over medium heat. Add onion and celery and sauté until soft and translucent, about 7 minutes. Add thyme leaves and sauté additional 1 minute.

4 ◆ Add onion mixture, cranberries and pecans to the cooked quinoa and toss until combined; add salt and pepper to taste. (Broth is already salty, so be careful when adding more salt.)

5 ◆ Fill each squash half with quinoa mixture. Drizzle with a bit of honey before serving, if desired. If you have stuffing left over, bring it to work for a delicious lunch.

Quinoa-Stuffed Squash with ▶
Pears and Cranberries

✦✦✦ Caramelized Onion Rice

This dish is a riff on the Middle Eastern staple mujaddara. Here, slivered almonds replace the traditional version's lentils.
Ⓟ Serves 4–6

1 cup basmati rice
3 tablespoons olive oil
2 onions, chopped
1 teaspoon salt
2 cloves garlic, chopped

1/2 teaspoon cumin
1/2 cup slivered almonds, toasted
1/4 cup chopped flat-leaf parsley (optional)

1 ✦ Cook rice according to package directions; remove from heat and set aside.

2 ✦ Meanwhile, heat oil in a medium pan over medium heat. Add onions and salt and cook, stirring occasionally, until browned, about 10 minutes. Add garlic and cumin and cook for an additional 2–3 minutes until fragrant; remove from heat.

3 ✦ Add onion mixture, toasted almonds and parsley (if using) to the cooked rice and stir well to combine.

✦✦✦ Warm Barley, Apple and Feta Salad

A burst of fresh parsley and lemon juice pair with sharp feta crumbles in this warm barley dish. The feta is really instrumental in tying the flavors together but can be omitted if serving with a meat meal. Ⓓ Ⓟ Serves 4

1 cup pearl barley
2 stalks celery, diced
1 green apple (e.g., Granny Smith), peeled and diced
2 tablespoons chopped flat-leaf parsley

1/2 cup crumbled feta cheese
1/4 cup lemon juice
3 tablespoons olive oil
2 teaspoons honey
Salt and freshly ground black pepper

1 ✦ Boil barley in large saucepan, partially covered, until tender, about 30 minutes. Meanwhile, chop celery, apple and parsley.

2 ✦ Drain barley and transfer, still warm, to a bowl. Add celery, apple, parsley and feta. In a small bowl, whisk together lemon juice, oil, honey and salt and pepper to taste; drizzle over salad and toss to combine. Serve warm or at room temperature.

Warm Barley, Apple and ▶
Feta Salad

Couscous with Dried Cherries and Mint

The beans, fruit and grains in this side dish offer the nutritional profile of a complete meal. **D P** Serves 6

TIP *Switch things up by substituting less common grains like wheat berries, spelt or farro in place of the couscous.*

1 1/2 cups Israeli couscous
1 15-ounce can rosa (pink) beans or white beans, rinsed and drained
1/2 cup red onion, halved and thinly sliced
1/2 cup dried cherries (or dried cranberries), chopped
5 tablespoons light olive oil

1/4 cup plus 1 tablespoon lemon juice
3 tablespoons honey
Salt and freshly ground black pepper
1/4 cup chopped mint
1/4 cup crumbled feta or goat cheese (optional)

1 ◆ Cook couscous according to package directions; remove from heat and set aside.

2 ◆ In a medium bowl, combine beans, onion and cherries. In a small bowl, whisk together oil, lemon juice, honey, salt and pepper to taste, mint and feta or goat cheese, if using.

3 ◆ Add couscous to the bean mixture and toss gently with about two thirds of the dressing until combined. Add additional dressing to taste. Tightly seal and refrigerate any leftover dressing.

◀ *Couscous with Dried Cherries and Mint*

❧◆❧ Lemony Spaghetti Pasta Salad

This tangy, lemon-infused pasta salad is destined to be a hit at your next potluck. For a tasty, nutrient-packed twist, try adding lightly steamed broccoli florets. **Ⓟ Serves 6**

1 1-pound package spaghetti (or angel hair or linguine pasta)
1/2 cup olive oil
2 cloves garlic, minced
2 shallots, diced
1/2 cup lemon juice (5–6 lemons)
Zest of two lemons
1/2 cup pine nuts, toasted

1 pint grape tomatoes, halved
1 16-ounce jar water-packed artichoke hearts, quartered
1/2 cup sliced black olives
1/4 cup chopped flat-leaf parsley
1 teaspoon dried basil
Sea salt and freshly ground black pepper

1 ◆ Cook spaghetti according to package directions; drain and set aside.

2 ◆ Heat oil in a large pan over medium heat. Add garlic and shallots and sauté, stirring regularly, until soft and fragrant, 2–3 minutes. Remove pan from heat and add lemon juice and zest.

3 ◆ Return spaghetti to the pot (or transfer to a large bowl) and pour lemon juice mixture over pasta; toss well to coat. Add pine nuts, tomatoes, artichoke hearts, olives, parsley, basil and salt and pepper to taste, tossing well to combine.

❧◆❧ Basil Two-Bean Salad

Honey, lime juice and fresh basil bring out the best in this summery two-bean salad. **Ⓟ Serves 6**

1/2 medium red onion, diced
2 teaspoons red wine vinegar
1 15-ounce can black beans, rinsed and drained
1 15-ounce can white beans (e.g. cannellini), rinsed and drained
3 ears of corn, kernels removed (or 2 cups canned white corn)

1 teaspoon balsamic vinegar
2 teaspoons lime zest
Juice of 2 limes
2 tablespoons honey
1/4 cup olive oil
1/2 cup basil leaves, finely chopped

1 ◦ In a small bowl, combine red onion and red wine vinegar and let sit for at least 10 minutes to allow the onion to mellow. In a medium bowl, combine black beans, white beans and corn; set aside.

2 ◦ Whisk together balsamic vinegar, lime zest and juice, honey and oil in a small bowl. Add basil and whisk again to combine. Stir red onion mixture into beans; drizzle with dressing and gently fold to combine. Cover and refrigerate until serving.

REMOVING CORN KERNELS

◆ ◆ ◆ ◆ ◆

Canned and frozen corn both work well in the colder months when corn is out of season. But when it comes to flavor and crunch, nothing beats fresh, in-season corn kernels.

To remove kernels, first take off the husk and silky threads surrounding the cob. Grasping the stem, stand the shucked corncob upright, tip resting on a cutting board. Hold the cob steady while using a sharp knife to make downward cuts along the cob. Work your way around the cob until all kernels are removed; gather kernels, rinse if desired and add to recipe. One medium-sized ear of corn yields about 3/4 cup kernels.

⋇◆⋊ Orzo and Pinto Bean Salad

Silky orzo and creamy pinto beans are a match made in side dish heaven. Take the leftovers with you to work for lunch.
Serves 4–6

1 cup orzo
1/3 cup red onion, diced
2 tablespoons lemon juice, divided
1 15-ounce can pinto beans, drained and rinsed
2 tablespoons chopped flat-leaf parsley
1 tablespoon dried oregano
2 tablespoons red wine vinegar

2 tablespoons olive oil
1 kirby cucumber, diced
1/2 cup pitted kalamata olives, halved
1 teaspoon lemon zest
1/2 teaspoon salt
1/4 teaspoon freshly ground black pepper
1 cup crumbled feta (optional)

1 ◦ Cook orzo according to package instructions. Transfer to a sieve and rinse under cold water to stop cooking; drain well and set aside. (At this point, orzo can be stored in an airtight container in the refrigerator for up to 2 days.)

2 ◦ In a small bowl, combine red onion and lemon juice and allow to sit for at least 10 minutes to allow the onion to mellow.

3 ◦ Meanwhile, in a large bowl toss the pinto beans, parsley, oregano, vinegar, oil, cucumber, olives, lemon zest, salt and pepper, stirring well to combine. Add the orzo, red onion mixture (with juices) and feta, if using, and gently fold to combine.

MAINS

Mains

The dinner table plays a fundamental role in Jewish life. No description of Shabbat would be complete without mention of the table—as the symbolic embodiment of the altar at the Holy Temple and as the physical center of our celebration. The table is the connector that brings people together in the glow of candlelight, wine and warm challah to eat, discuss, sing and simply enjoy one another's company.

◆ ◆ ◆

The rest of the week, of course, is typically more hectic than Friday night. With everyone operating on different timetables—school, work, soccer practice, evening meetings—managing to eat dinner together feels like a constant struggle. There will most likely be nights when a sandwich eaten on the run plays stand-in for a sit-down supper. Still, when all the pieces fall into place, even for 30 minutes a few times a week, we welcome a bit of Shabbat dinner's warmth into our regular routine.

◆ ◆ ◆

As the Latvian proverb wisely points out, the right dinner companions can make a meal feel special. Delicious food doesn't hurt either. The recipes in this section include chicken, meat and fish dishes—like **Sesame Seed Chicken Cutlets** *(page 143)*, **Beer-Braised Beef** *(page 154)*, **Dried Cherry Burgers** *(page 160)* and **Brown Sugar-Glazed Salmon** *(page 147)*—that come together quickly and are destined to become family classics. You will also find plenty of meatless mains, from **Ginger Sesame Baked Tempeh** *(page 157)* to eggy **Shakshuka** *(page 163)* and **Quasado** *(page 161)*, which satisfy vegetarians and omnivores alike. And with hearty pasta dishes like **Roasted Butternut Squash and Red Onion Penne** *(page 166)* and **Ricotta-Stuffed Shells** *(page 167)* rounding things out, finding time for nourishing, family-friendly dinners can become an everyday reality.

PAGES **138–139:** *Grilled Lamb Chops with Mint Chimichurri, recipe, page 151*

❧◆❧ Maple-Glazed Chicken Teriyaki

Your entire household will enjoy this fast, inexpensive dinner. Start marinating the chicken the night before or in the morning so the dish comes together in minutes at suppertime. Experiment with different flavors in the marinade—try adding fresh herbs, vinegars or dried spices. Serve over rice or soba noodles. Ⓜ **Serves 4–6**

*4 skinless, boneless chicken
    breasts
1/2 cup tamari or soy sauce
4 tablespoons maple syrup
2 cloves garlic, minced*

*2 teaspoons grated fresh ginger
3 tablespoons vegetable oil
Toasted cashews and chopped
    scallions for garnish
    (optional)*

1 ◆ If chicken breasts are thick, either butterfly them and then cut in half or cover them with plastic wrap and pound them gently with a meat tenderizer until each breast is about 1/2-inch thick. Then cut the breasts into 2-inch square pieces.

2 ◆ In a small bowl, whisk the tamari or soy sauce, maple syrup, garlic and ginger together. Put the chicken in a baking dish and pour the sauce over. Move the pieces around to thoroughly coat chicken. Cover and marinate the chicken in the refrigerator for at least 15 minutes and up to 24 hours.

3 ◆ Heat the oil in a wide, deep sauté pan over medium heat. Using a slotted spoon or fork, add the chicken to the pan without the marinade (so that the chicken will get crispy). Set the remaining marinade aside. Cook chicken for 5 minutes and then turn over each piece. Continue to cook another 5 minutes, until pieces are browned on both sides and thoroughly cooked.

4 ◆ Add the remaining marinade to the pan, turn the heat down to low and cook for a minute or two longer, until most of the marinade is absorbed. Transfer chicken to a serving platter and garnish with cashews and scallions, if desired. Store the chicken in a sealed container in the refrigerator for up to 3 days.

✄◆✄ Sesame Seed Chicken Cutlets

Fried chicken cutlets are a simple, go-to dish for many Jewish chefs. This version gets a punch of wholesome and tasty goodness thanks to ground flax seeds and toasted sesame seeds. Ⓜ **Serves 4**

4 skinless, boneless chicken breasts
Seasonings: kosher salt, freshly ground black pepper, onion powder, garlic powder and chili powder
2 large eggs
1 1/2 cups unseasoned breadcrumbs
1/4 cup ground flax seeds (flax seed meal)
1/2 cup sesame seeds, toasted
Vegetable oil for frying
Lemon wedges for garnish

1 ◆ Butterfly chicken breasts but do not cut all the way through the breasts. Season both sides of the chicken with salt, pepper, onion powder, garlic powder and chili powder to taste, approximately 1/4 teaspoon of each.

2 ◆ In a small bowl, beat the eggs and then transfer to a large plate. On a separate large plate, mix the breadcrumbs, ground flax seeds and toasted sesame seeds.

3 ◆ Heat the oil in a medium sauté pan (use enough oil so that it comes halfway up the sides of the pan). Dip the chicken breasts in the egg followed by the crumb mixture. Shake off excess crumbs and pan fry. (You should hear a sizzle, otherwise the oil is not hot enough.) Do this in batches if necessary in order to not crowd the pan.

4 ◆ When the chicken pieces are golden brown and crispy, about 5 minutes per side, transfer to a plate lined with paper towels to absorb excess oil. Squeeze a bit of lemon juice over the breasts before serving, and garnish with lemon wedges if desired.

HOW TO BUTTERFLY CHICKEN
◆ ◆ ◆ ◆ ◆

Use the tip of a chef's knife—also called a French knife—and, starting at the thickest part of the breast, begin cutting down the length of the side of the breast. Keep your knife parallel to the cutting board and carefully slice the breast in half widthwise almost to the other edge. Do not cut all the way through. You should now have what looks like an opened book. Either cut the butterflied chicken in half or leave as a book, depending on recipe.

✦✦ Miso Ginger Chicken

Savory miso paste and a fiery kick of ginger: chicken breasts never had it so good! Serve this dish alongside tender **Braised Fennel** (page 120) and jasmine rice. Ⓜ **Serves 4**

3/4 cup miso paste (available at health food stores and Asian groceries)
1/2 cup sugar
1/2 cup chicken broth
1/4 cup rice wine vinegar

3 tablespoons soy sauce
2 tablespoons minced fresh ginger
4 skinless, boneless chicken breasts
2 tablespoons olive oil

1 ◆ Combine all ingredients except chicken and oil in a medium bowl and whisk to combine; don't worry if the miso clumps a bit. Add chicken to the marinade, coat thoroughly and let sit in the refrigerator for at least 10 minutes.

2 ◆ Heat oil in a large sauté pan over medium heat. Lift chicken breasts out of the marinade one by one, letting excess drip off, and transfer to pan. Repeat, making sure not to overcrowd the pan. Cook 5–7 minutes per side, until well browned and cooked through. Transfer chicken to a plate to cool, about 5 minutes.

3 ◆ Meanwhile, add any remaining marinade to pan and cook, stirring continuously, until sauce reduces, about 5 minutes (sauce should be thick enough to coat a wooden spoon). Spoon sauce over chicken before serving.

◀ *Miso Ginger Chicken shown with Braised Fennel, recipe, page 120*

✳◆✳ Herb-Roasted Chicken

The aroma of chicken roasting in the oven evokes a primitive, soul-satisfying response. After mastering the basic technique, play around by adding fresh cloves of garlic or tossing some chopped root vegetables in the bottom of the roasting pan. Pair this chicken with either the **Thyme-Roasted Root Vegetables** (page 123) or **Grilled Herbed Potatoes** (page 122). Ⓜ **Serves 4**

5 pounds cut-up chicken pieces, white and dark meat	*Mix and match herbs (optional):* *1 tablespoon fresh rosemary,*
Salt and freshly ground black pepper	*1 tablespoon fresh thyme,* *1 tablespoon fresh oregano (for*
1/4 cup olive oil	*dried herbs, use 1 teaspoon each)*

1 ◆ Preheat oven to 400 degrees. Thoroughly wash all chicken pieces, pat dry and trim excess fat.

2 ◆ Place chicken pieces in a large baking dish or roasting pan. Season with salt and pepper to taste, any herbs you choose and then drizzle with enough oil to completely coat the chicken, approximately 1/4 cup. Use your hands to turn over all the chicken pieces, evenly distributing oil and any herbs you are using.

3 ◆ Roast chicken, skin sides up, for approximately 1 hour, basting after 20 minutes and after 40 minutes.

✳◆✳ Pomegranate Chicken

This adaptation of fesenjen, a traditional dish enjoyed by Persian Jews, maintains the original recipe's sweet and savory flavor but gets dinner on the table in a fraction of the time. Serve it over Israeli couscous or your favorite grain. Ⓜ **Serves 4**

5 skinless, boneless chicken thighs	*1 1/2 cups pomegranate juice (not from concentrate)*
Salt and freshly ground black pepper	
1/4 cup vegetable oil	*2 tablespoons honey*
1 large onion, diced	*1/2 cup chopped mint or flat-leaf parsley*
3/4 cup pistachios or walnuts, chopped	*1/4 cup pomegranate seeds for garnish*
1 1/2 teaspoons cinnamon	

1 ◆ Season the chicken with salt and pepper to taste. In a large sauté pan, heat the oil over medium heat. Add chicken and cook, turning once, until browned, about 8 minutes total. Transfer chicken to a plate.

2 ◆ Add the onion to the skillet and cook until lightly caramelized, 5–6 minutes. Add the pistachios or walnuts and cinnamon and stir, cooking another 2 minutes until the mixture becomes fragrant.

3 ◆ Return the chicken and any juices to the pan, add the pomegranate juice and honey and simmer over medium heat until the chicken is cooked through, about 10 minutes; transfer chicken to a serving platter.

4 ◆ Continue cooking sauce, stirring occasionally, until slightly thickened, about 3 minutes. Stir in the mint and then pour sauce over the chicken. Garnish with more chopped mint and pomegranate seeds, if desired.

Brown Sugar-Glazed Salmon

While you could bake this salmon dish, broiling allows the brown sugar to caramelize, giving the fish a beautiful, rich color. Ⓓ Ⓟ **Serves 4**

1/2 cup brown sugar
4 tablespoons butter or non-hydrogenated margarine, melted
2 cloves garlic, chopped
3 tablespoons tamari or soy sauce
2 tablespoons lemon juice
2 tablespoons dry white wine
Salt and freshly ground black pepper
4 salmon fillets
Toasted sesame seeds (optional)

1 ◆ Combine sugar, butter or margarine, garlic, tamari or soy sauce, lemon juice, wine and salt and pepper to taste in a small bowl. Whisk until sugar in dissolved, then set marinade aside.

2 ◆ Wash salmon and pat dry; place fillets in a baking dish. Pour marinade over fish, cover with plastic wrap and marinate for at least 1 hour in the refrigerator (or up to 6).

3 ◆ Preheat broiler. Transfer salmon, skin side down, to rimmed baking sheet lined with aluminum foil that has been coated with cooking spray. Scrape off garlic bits from atop fillets so they do not burn. Broil 10 minutes per inch of thickness. Sprinkle toasted sesame seeds over fillets before serving, if desired.

MAKING BROWN SUGAR

Out of brown sugar? Avoid an extra trip to the store by making it at home. Brown sugar is essentially regular sugar plus molasses (3.5% for light and 6.5% for dark). To make your own, simply put white sugar in a bowl, add molasses (1–2 teaspoons per cup of sugar) and stir well to combine. Within a minute or two, the sugar will darken and take on a slightly sticky consistency, exactly like brown sugar.

❧❖❧ Citrus Cod with White Wine

Orange, lime and lemon juice team up to add bright citrus flavor to this baked fish ⓟ **Serves 3–4**

➤TIP *Use a wine you would like to drink in this dish, then serve the extra with dinner.*

1 1/2 pounds cod fillets (or any white fish)
1/2 cup white wine
Juice of 1 orange
Juice of 2 limes
Juice of 1 lemon
1/4 cup olive oil
1 teaspoon lemon zest

1 teaspoon orange zest
4 cloves garlic, minced
1 shallot, minced
3 scallions, thinly sliced, plus more for garnish
1 teaspoon kosher salt
Freshly ground black pepper
1 yellow onion, sliced

1 ◆ Preheat oven to 350 degrees. Rinse fish, pat dry and place in a glass baking dish.

2 ◆ Whisk together wine and citrus juices. Add oil in a slow stream, whisking until emulsified. Stir in zests.

3 ◆ Pour wine and citrus dressing on top of fish. Sprinkle garlic, shallot and scallions on fish and season with salt and pepper to taste. Arrange onions around fish. If desired, add a few thin rounds of one or more of the citrus fruits to the dish for color.

4 ◆ Bake for 20–25 minutes, until fish is cooked through. Serve topped with additional scallions, if desired.

Citrus Cod with White Wine shown with Lemony Asparagus recipe, page 117 ▶

❈◆❈ Tilapia Four Ways

These basic cooking instructions and ingredients work well for many types of fish: Feel free to substitute snapper, cod, halibut or salmon for the tilapia. **Ⓓ Ⓟ Serves 4**

4 tilapia fillets, approximately 1-inch thick
6 tablespoons olive oil, divided

Salt and freshly ground black pepper

1 ◆ Preheat oven to 400 degrees. Rinse fillets and dry them very thoroughly (there should be no water clinging to the fish).

2 ◆ Drizzle 3 tablespoons oil into the bottom of a glass baking dish. Season each side of the fillet with salt and pepper to taste and place in the dish; drizzle the remaining oil over the fillets.

3 ◆ Top each fillet with desired topping (see below); bake for approximately 20 minutes or until fish is cooked through.

WALNUT AND PARSLEY: Combine the following in a bowl: 1/2 cup panko breadcrumbs, 1/2 cup chopped walnuts, juice of 1 lemon, 1/2 cup chopped flat-leaf parsley, 1/4 cup melted butter or non-hydrogenated margarine and salt and freshly ground black pepper to taste.

TOMATO AND SCALLION: In a sauté pan, heat 2 tablespoons olive oil over medium heat. Add 1 cup seeded and chopped plum tomatoes, 1/4 cup chopped scallions, 1/2 cup chopped flat-leaf parsley, 1 teaspoon dried dill and 1 teaspoon lemon zest and salt and pepper to taste; sauté lightly until slightly softened, about 5 minutes. Remove from heat and stir in 1/2 cup panko breadcrumbs.

SPINACH AND SHALLOT: In a sauté pan, melt 1/4 cup butter or non-hydrogenated margarine over medium heat. Add 2 minced shallots, 1 cup roughly chopped baby spinach, 1/2 cup chopped flat-leaf parsley, 1 teaspoon lemon zest, 1 teaspoon dried dill and salt and pepper to taste. Sauté lightly until spinach is wilted, about 4 minutes. Remove from heat and stir in 1/2 cup panko breadcrumbs.

SWEET ONION AND PISTACHIO: In a sauté pan, heat 3 tablespoons olive oil over medium heat. Add 1/2 cup chopped sweet onion such as Vidalia, 1/2 cup chopped flat-leaf parsley, 1 tablespoon lemon zest and salt and pepper to taste. Sauté until onion is soft and translucent, about 5 minutes. Remove from heat and stir in 1/2 cup chopped pistachio nuts.

Grilled Lamb Chops with
Mint Chimichurri, photo
pages 138–139

⋊◆⋉ Grilled Lamb Chops with Mint Chimichurri

Fresh mint chimichurri adds a spicy Argentinean spin to the iconic pairing of lamb and mint jelly. The chimichurri also tastes delicious spooned over grilled chicken, tofu or vegetables. **Ⓜ Serves 4**

FOR THE CHIMICHURRI:
1/4 cup chopped flat-leaf parsley
3 tablespoons red wine vinegar
4 cloves garlic, minced
2 tablespoons chopped cilantro
2 tablespoons chopped mint
1 teaspoon crushed red pepper
    flakes

Kosher salt and freshly ground
    black pepper
1/3 cup olive oil

FOR THE LAMB CHOPS:
12 baby lamb chops
1/3 cup olive oil
Salt and freshly ground black
    pepper

1 ◆ In a food processor, pulse the parsley, vinegar, garlic, cilantro, mint, red pepper flakes and salt and pepper to taste. Add the oil in a stream and process until the chimichurri is smooth. Transfer sauce to a bowl and let sit for at least 20 minutes to let the flavors develop. (You can make the sauce ahead, refrigerating it overnight and bringing it to room temperature before serving.)

2 ◆ Meanwhile, prepare the lamb chops. Rub oil and salt and pepper to taste onto the lamb chops, then cook either on an outdoor grill or inside on a grill pan over medium heat to your desired doneness (about 4 minutes per side for medium rare). For best results, only flip the chops once. Serve the chops alongside the chimichurri sauce, in a serving dish.

FRENCHING LAMB CHOPS
◆◆◆◆◆

For everyday presentation, Frenching lamb chops may seem unnecessary. But, if you have an extra few minutes, are entertaining or want to flex your gourmet muscle, try Frenching either individual chops or a rack of lamb.

To do so, start with a small, very sharp paring or boning knife and scrape away the meat and fat attached to the bone. Begin with the fat surrounding the chop and scrape upward toward the tip of the bone. If any bits of flesh or fat remain on the bone, wrap your hand in a dishtowel and pull up on the bone, wiping it clean.

❖❖ Pepper Steak

Pineapple juice adds sweet and sour flavor to this easy-to-prepare Chinese restaurant classic. Serve over white or brown rice. Ⓜ **Serves 4**

1/3 cup soy sauce
1/3 cup pineapple juice
1/2 teaspoon garlic powder
1/4 teaspoon ginger powder
3 tablespoons brown sugar
Salt and freshly ground
*   black pepper*
1 tablespoon olive oil

1 1/2 pounds skirt steak, trimmed
*   of excess fat*
3 bell peppers (green, red and
*   yellow), cut into 1/4-inch sticks*
1/2 pound fresh button mushrooms,
*   sliced*
1 cup plum tomatoes, seeded
*   and chopped*
Toasted sesame seeds (optional)

1 ❖ In a medium bowl, combine soy sauce, pineapple juice, garlic powder, ginger powder, brown sugar and salt and pepper to taste; set aside.

2 ❖ In a sauté pan or cast-iron skillet, heat oil over medium heat. Cook the steak, about 5 minutes per side, until browned. Remove steak from pan and let sit for at least 5 minutes to seal in juices. Then, slice steak into thin 1/4-inch strips; set aside.

3 ❖ In the same pan, sauté the peppers and mushrooms until soft, about 10 minutes. Add browned meat, tomatoes and sauce and simmer until meat is cooked through, just a few minutes. Garnish with toasted sesame seeds, if desired.

Pepper Steak ▶

❖◆❖ Beer-Braised Beef

Carbonated beer bubbles help tenderize the beef in this dish, producing a slow-simmered, deeply flavored meal. Serve with **Garlicky Sautéed Greens** (page 116) and boiled new potatoes or egg noodles. Ⓜ **Serves 4–6**

*4 pounds beef chuck, trimmed and
    cut into 1 1/2 inch pieces
Salt and freshly ground black pepper
4 cloves garlic, chopped
1 large onion, diced*

*2 stalks celery, diced
1 carrot, diced
1 bottle beer
1 teaspoon tomato paste
Low-sodium beef broth*

1 ◆   Heat a large sauté pan over medium-high heat. Season pieces of beef with salt and pepper and sear in the pan without overcrowding until all sides are brown. (You may have to do this in two batches.) Remove beef and set aside.

2 ◆ Add garlic to pan and cook over medium heat until fragrant, about 1 minute. Add some water and scrape up the fond (the flavorful bits that have stuck to the bottom of the pan). Then add the onion, celery and carrot and cook until onion is soft, about 5 minutes.

3 ◆ Add beer and stir until the fond has been completely incorporated into the liquid. Stir in tomato paste and cook for 5 minutes.

4 ◆ Return the beef to the pan and add enough broth to come about halfway up the meat. (If your pan is too small, split the vegetable and beer mixture between two pans, then add the beef to both.) Cover the pan and simmer until a fork will easily slide in and out of a piece of meat, approximately 45 minutes. (You can cut the beef smaller if you want to speed up cooking time.) If the liquid has a loose consistency, remove the meat when it is done and continue to reduce the liquid to your desired consistency, and return the meat to the pan to warm up before serving.

⋈◆⋈ Pan-Fried Tofu with Peanut Sauce

Velvety peanut sauce makes an ideal topping for crispy fried tofu. Serve this dish with lime wedges to squeeze on top. Pair with an Asian-inspired side like **Ginger Sesame Green Beans** (page 117). **ⓟ Serves 3–4**

FOR TOFU:
4 tablespoons vegetable oil
1 package extra-firm tofu, water pressed out and cut into 1/2-inch pieces
Salt

FOR PEANUT SAUCE:
2/3 cup peanut butter (creamy or crunchy)

1 tablespoon soy sauce
2 tablespoons brown sugar or maple syrup
1/2 teaspoon red pepper flakes
2 tablespoons lime juice
1 1/2 teaspoons sesame oil
1/4–1/2 cup warm water
1/4 cup chopped cilantro (optional)

1 ◆ *Fry the tofu:* Heat oil in a heavy sauté pan or cast-iron skillet over medium heat. Add tofu pieces, sprinkle with salt and brown, 6–7 minutes. Flip pieces and fry an additional 4–5 minutes. Transfer to paper towels and cool slightly.

2 ◆ Combine peanut butter, soy sauce, brown sugar or maple syrup, red pepper flakes, lime juice and sesame oil in a medium bowl. Add water slowly, stirring to combine until you reach desired consistency and thickness. Stir in cilantro, if using, and adjust any other ingredients to taste. Serve in a bowl alongside the fired tofu.

PRESSING WATER OUT OF TOFU
◆ ◆ ◆ ◆ ◆

Whenever you are pan-frying or baking tofu, start with an extra-firm variety and press out any excess water before cooking. After removing the tofu from its package and discarding any liquid, wrap the block in a layer of paper towels, followed by a clean dishtowel. Lay the wrapped tofu on the counter and place a dinner plate, can of beans or other heavy object on top. Let sit for 10–15 minutes, then unwrap and slice.

Ginger Sesame Baked Tempeh shown with Ginger Sesame Green Beans, recipe, page 117

❈◆❈ Ginger Sesame Baked Tempeh

Pair this dish with **Ginger Sesame Green Beans** (page 117) or **Lemony Asparagus** (page 117) and **Colcannon** (page 127) for a well-rounded and delicious vegetarian supper. If you prefer, substitute extra-firm tofu for the tempeh. ℗ **Serves 3–4**

2 tablespoons tamari or soy sauce	*2 teaspoons sesame oil*
1 teaspoon cider vinegar	*1/4 cup orange juice*
2 1/2 teaspoons finely chopped fresh ginger	*1 8-ounce package tempeh, cut into 1/4-inch strips or triangles*
1/2 teaspoon garlic powder	*1/4 cup toasted sesame seeds (optional)*
2 tablespoons honey	

1 ◆ In a medium bowl, whisk together tamari or soy sauce, vinegar, ginger, garlic powder, honey, sesame oil and orange juice. Add the tempeh and marinate at room temperature, turning occasionally, 15–20 minutes.

2 ◆ Preheat oven to 375 degrees. Transfer marinated tempeh pieces and any remaining juice to an 8 x 8-inch baking dish, making sure the tempeh pieces are not touching. Bake for 12 minutes, then flip pieces and bake an additional 12–15 minutes until tempeh is browned and the marinade has reduced to a sticky sauce. Serve topped with sesame seeds, if desired.

TEMPEH
❖❖❖❖❖

Tempeh is a traditional Indonesian food made from soybeans that have been cultured and pressed into cakes. Its firm texture and nutty flavor makes it a delicious alternative to meat, and the fermentation process used to make tempeh allows the final product to retain higher amounts of protein and vitamins than tofu.

Tempeh is widely available in health food stores and increasingly available at supermarkets. A note on freshness: tempeh will occasionally have darkened areas, especially around the edges. This coloration is a result of the culturing process and not an indication of spoilage.

✖◆✖ Cumin and Cilantro Burgers

These piquant burgers might just become your new summer favorite. If desired, substitute ground lamb for half of the beef. Serve with a zesty, refreshing salad like the **Honey Sesame Slaw** (page 63). **Ⓜ Serves 6–8**

2 pounds ground beef
1/4 cup chopped cilantro
1/4 cup scallions, thinly sliced
2 cloves garlic, minced
1 teaspoon cumin
1 teaspoon chili powder
1 teaspoon onion powder

Kosher salt and freshly ground
*   black pepper*
Hamburger buns
Garnishes (optional): lettuce,
*   tomato slices, onion, ketchup,*
*   mustard, salsa*

1 ◆ Preheat outdoor grill or grill pan to medium heat. In a large bowl, combine beef, cilantro, scallions, garlic, cumin, chili powder, onion powder and salt and pepper to taste. Mix thoroughly with hands.

2 ◆ Divide mixture into 6–8 portions depending on desired size and form into patties; make a slight indentation in the center of each to stop the patties from puffing up while cooking.

3 ◆ Grill burgers until browned and crispy on both sides, about 5 minutes per side, or according to your desired doneness. Place on a toasted bun and top with any garnishes you desire.

Dried Cherry Burgers [background], ▶
recipe, page 160, and Cumin and
Cilantro Burgers [foreground]

❖◆❖ Dried Cherry Burgers

The sweet-tart flavor of dried cherries perfectly complements ground beef. Try serving these burgers alongside **Grilled Tzimmes** (page 125). **Ⓜ Serves 4–6**

1 pound ground beef	1 tablespoon balsamic vinegar
1/4 cup minced shallots	2 teaspoons Dijon mustard
1/4 cup dried cherries or cranberries, finely chopped	Salt and freshly ground black pepper
1/2 cup breadcrumbs, preferably whole wheat	Hamburger buns
1 clove garlic, minced	Garnishes (optional): ketchup, citrus marmalade, sweet onion slices, lettuce
2 tablespoons chopped basil	

1 ◆ Preheat outdoor grill or grill pan to medium heat. In a large bowl, combine beef, shallots, cherries or cranberries, breadcrumbs, garlic, basil, vinegar, mustard and salt and pepper to taste. Mix thoroughly with hands.

2 ◆ Divide mixture into 4–6 portions depending on desired size and form into patties; make a slight indentation in the center of each to stop the patties from puffing up while cooking.

3 ◆ Grill patties until browned and cooked through, about 5 minutes per side, or according to your desired doneness. Place on a toasted bun and top with any garnishes you desire.

❖◆❖ Portobello Burger

These vegetarian-friendly burgers are incredibly simple to prepare and packed with satisfying "meaty" flavor. Serve them with crispy **Sweet Potato Fries** (page 125) or **Baked Onion Rings** (page 126). **Ⓓ Ⓟ Serves 4**

1/2 cup balsamic vinegar	4 slices cheddar cheese— or pepper jack, fontina or smoked mozzarella (optional)
1 cup olive oil	
1 teaspoon salt	
Freshly ground black pepper	
4 medium Portobello mushrooms, stems removed and rinsed	Toppings (optional): lettuce, tomato slices, mustard, pickles, avocado, roasted red peppers
4 hamburger buns or ciabatta rolls	

1 ◆ In a bowl, whisk together vinegar, oil, salt and pepper to taste; transfer vinaigrette to a baking dish. Place mushrooms in the vinaigrette and marinate for 15 minutes, flipping halfway through.

2 ◆ Heat a heavy-bottomed sauté pan or cast-iron skillet over medium-high heat. Add mushrooms, top down, and cook for 4–5 minutes until a nice crust forms on the top of the cap. Flip and cook for an additional 4–5 minutes. Turn off heat, add cheese slices if using, and cover until cheese melts, 2–3 minutes.

3 ◆ Transfer to buns and garnish with desired toppings.

✳◆✳ Quasado

Seattle is home to a large population of Sephardic Jews, the first of whom arrived from Turkey in 1904. This dish is very popular in the community, which today numbers around 5,000 people. This recipe is not dependent on exact ingredients, so try using different cheeses such as feta or goat cheese. ⓓ **Serves 8**

2 teaspoons vegetable oil
10 large eggs
2 cups baby spinach
2 tablespoons chopped fresh basil
  or 2 teaspoons dried basil
1 cup grated mozzarella cheese
3/4 cup grated Parmesan cheese,
  plus more for sprinkling

1/2 cup unseasoned breadcrumbs
  or matza meal
1/2 teaspoon garlic powder
1/4 teaspoon red pepper flakes
1/4 teaspoon kosher or sea salt
Freshly ground black pepper

1 ◆ Preheat oven to 375 degrees. Grease a 9 x 13-inch baking dish with oil; set aside. In a medium bowl, beat the eggs. Stir in the spinach, basil, cheeses, breadcrumbs, garlic, red pepper flakes, salt and pepper to taste.

2 ◆ Pour egg and spinach mixture into the greased baking dish and spread evenly. Sprinkle with additional Parmesan.

3 ◆ Cover very loosely with foil and bake for 15 minutes; uncover and bake until edges are browned and Parmesan is crispy, another 5–10 minutes. Season with additional salt and pepper to taste before serving.

❊◆❊ Shakshuka

Originally from North Africa, this dish is a favorite in Israel for breakfast, lunch or dinner. Whole eggs simmered in tomato sauce makes a quick, nourishing dinner to mop up with crusty bread. Ⓟ **Serves 2–3**

2 tablespoons olive oil
1 small onion, chopped
1 red pepper, seeded and chopped
1 28-ounce can whole, peeled
  plum tomatoes
5 cloves garlic, diced
2 teaspoons salt

1 teaspoon paprika
1/8 teaspoon cayenne powder
2 heaping teaspoons tomato paste
1/4 cup vegetable oil
4–6 large eggs
Red pepper flakes and za'atar for
  garnish (optional)

1 ◆ Heat oil in a 12-inch sauté pan or cast-iron skillet. Add onions and pepper and sauté until softened, about 6 minutes.

2 ◆ Pour tomatoes and juice into a bowl and squeeze gently with your hands to break them up. Add crushed tomatoes (with juice) to the pan along with garlic, salt, paprika, cayenne powder, tomato paste and oil; cover. Bring to a simmer, uncover and stir occasionally until mixture thickens slightly, 25–30 minutes.

3 ◆ Break desired number of eggs directly into pan, over the tomatoes. Cover and continue to cook until eggs are set, 5–6 minutes, carefully basting the eggs once or twice with sauce. Serve hot, sprinkled with red pepper flakes and za'atar, if desired.

◀ *Shakshuka*

✖◆✖ Cauliflower and Caramelized Onion Quiche

You can use store-bought piecrust for this quiche and omit the first and fourth steps, but homemade crust is surprisingly simple, and the taste is worth the extra effort. Try swapping out the cauliflower for other flavor combinations like spinach and halved cherry tomatoes or sautéed mushrooms and grated cheddar. ① **Serves 6–8**

FOR CRUST:
1 1/2 cups all-purpose flour
1 teaspoon sugar
1 teaspoon salt
1/2 cup (1 stick) cold unsalted butter,
*   cut into pieces*
4 tablespoons ice water

FOR QUICHE:
2 tablespoons olive oil
2 medium onions, halved and thinly sliced
1/4 teaspoon salt
1/2 head cauliflower, cut into small florets
6 large eggs
1/2 cup milk
1/2 teaspoon dried thyme
1/4 teaspoon red pepper flakes
Pinch of nutmeg
Salt and freshly ground black pepper
1/2 cup shredded cheddar cheese

1 ◆ *Make the crust:* Combine flour, sugar and salt in a large bowl. Add butter and, using your fingers, mix it into the flour until the mixture resembles coarse crumbs. While you work, bring flour from the bottom of the bowl up to meet the butter. Add ice water to the dough and stir with a wooden spoon to combine. If the mixture is too dry, add an additional tablespoon of water. (This dough can also be made by pulsing ingredients in a food processor until desired consistency is reached.) Using your hands, press the dough into a circle, then flatten into a disk. Wrap tightly in plastic and refrigerate while you make the filling.

2 ◆ Heat oil in a sauté pan or cast-iron skillet over medium-high heat. Add onions and salt and cook, stirring occasionally, until onions are browned, 8–10 minutes. Add cauliflower and cook until florets soften and brown, about 7 minutes.

3 ◆ Meanwhile, in a medium bowl, whisk together the eggs, milk, thyme, red pepper flakes, nutmeg and additional salt and pepper to taste. Set aside.

4 ◆ On a floured surface, roll out the crust into an 11-inch circle. Drape over a 9-inch pie dish, gently pressing dough flat against the bottom and sides, allowing excess to hang over the sides. Using a sharp knife, cut off excess dough; take a fork and press the rim of the pie dish to create creases.

5 ◆ Preheat oven to 375 degrees. Spread cauliflower and onion mixture around the bottom of the pie dish and sprinkle with cheese. Pour egg mixture over the onions and cheese and bake until set, 40–45 minutes. Cool slightly before serving.

✄◆✄ Zucchini Ricotta Tart

S erve this impressive (but deceptively simple) tart as the vegetarian main at your next dinner party. Ⓓ Serves 4

1 8 x 8-inch square puff pastry, thawed
2/3 cup ricotta cheese
Zest of 1 lemon
1/2 cup grated Parmesan cheese, plus more for sprinkling

Salt and freshly ground black pepper
1 zucchini (green or yellow), sliced as thinly as possible
1/4 cup pitted kalamata olives, halved
Handful of mint leaves, cut into ribbons

1 ◆ Preheat oven to 350 degrees. Line a baking sheet with parchment paper or foil. Unroll the thawed puffy pastry according to the package directions and place on sheet.

2 ◆ In a small bowl, mix the ricotta, lemon zest and Parmesan. Add salt and pepper to taste. Spread mixture onto puff pastry, leaving a 1/4-inch border around the edges.

3 ◆ Layer zucchini slices in slightly overlapping rows, again leaving the 1/4-inch border. Sprinkle with olive halves and top with additional Parmesan.

4 ◆ Bake for 35–40 minutes until golden at the edges and pastry is puffed up and crisp. Sprinkle with mint before serving. Slice and serve warm or at room temperature.

CHIFFONADING HERBS

● ● ● ● ●

Chiffonade is a knife technique used to produce thin, uniform ribbons from flat leafy greens like fresh herbs. Start with a bunch of washed and dried leaves (e.g., basil) and stack them together. Lay the stack flat on a cutting board and, starting at one end, roll the leaves tightly (it should resemble a jelly roll). Hold the roll firmly in place with one hand; with the other hand, begin to cut thin strips using a sharp knife and working your way across the roll.

❧◆❧ Roasted Butternut Squash and Red Onion Penne

This dish, which honors the flavors of fall, comes together while the squash and red onion are roasting. Ⓓ Ⓟ **Serves 4**

➔**TIP** *Feel free to swap out your favorite winter squash for the butternut.*

1 small butternut squash, peeled and chopped into 1/2-inch pieces

1 large red onion, cut into 1/4-inch chunks

4 tablespoons olive oil, divided

1 1/2 tablespoons balsamic vinegar

4 teaspoons dried thyme, divided

Salt and freshly ground black pepper

1 pound penne pasta (regular or whole wheat)

1/3 cup hazelnuts (or pecans), toasted and roughly chopped

3 ounces goat cheese, crumbled (optional)

1 ◆ Preheat oven to 400 degrees. In a large bowl, combine squash, red onion, 2 tablespoons oil, vinegar, 2 teaspoons thyme and salt and pepper to taste; toss well to thoroughly coat vegetables.

2 ◆ Spread squash and onion mixture onto a rimmed baking sheet and roast until squash softens and onion begins to caramelize, 30–35 minutes.

3 ◆ Meanwhile, set a pot of water over high heat; once boiling, drop in pasta and cook according to package directions until al dente. Drain pasta in a colander and transfer to a large bowl.

4 ◆ Stir remaining oil and thyme along with salt and pepper to taste into pasta. Transfer squash and onion mixture to the bowl along with hazelnuts and goat cheese, if using, and gently fold into pasta.

⋊◆⋉ Ricotta-Stuffed Shells

Creamy ricotta and zucchini make a hearty filling for this pasta casserole. Ⓓ **Serves 6–8**

1 12-ounce package jumbo shells pasta
1 tablespoon olive oil
2 cloves garlic, minced
6 cups shredded zucchini (about 3 medium zucchinis)
1 teaspoon salt
1/2 teaspoon freshly ground black pepper

1 teaspoon dried basil
1 15-ounce container ricotta cheese
1 cup grated Parmesan cheese, divided
3 tablespoons chopped dill
1 24-ounce jar marinara sauce

1 ◆ Cook pasta according to package directions until al dente; rinse, drain and set aside.

2 ◆ Heat oil in a large sauté pan over medium-high heat. Add garlic, zucchini, salt, pepper and basil and cook until tender and zucchini liquid is mostly evaporated, about 7 minutes. Turn off heat; let cool slightly, then stir in ricotta, 1/2 cup of Parmesan and dill.

3 ◆ Preheat oven to 375 degrees. Spread 3/4 cup tomato sauce in the bottom of a shallow 4-quart baking dish. Spoon a rounded tablespoon of the zucchini-cheese mixture into each shell, and layer shells into bottom of the dish.

4 ◆ Spoon remaining sauce over and in between shells and sprinkle leftover Parmesan on top. Cover with aluminum foil and bake for 25 minutes; uncover and bake an additional 5–7 minutes, until Parmesan is browned and sauce is bubbling.

✄✦✄ Farfalle with Mushrooms and Goat Cheese

Fresh goat cheese melts beautifully into pasta for a quick and tasty sauce. Ⓓ **Serves 4**

3/4 pound farfalle (bow tie pasta)
3 tablespoons butter or olive oil
2 medium onions, chopped
1/8 teaspoon salt
1/2 teaspoon sugar
4 Portobello mushrooms, stems
    removed and sliced into
    1/8-inch strips

3 cloves garlic, chopped
6 ounces goat cheese
1/4 cup milk
1/3 cup grated Parmesan cheese
1 small bunch diced chives,
    divided
Freshly ground black pepper

1 ◆ Cook farfalle according to package directions until al dente; drain and set aside.

2 ◆ Meanwhile, heat butter in a large sauté pan over medium heat. Add onions, salt and sugar and cook, stirring occasionally, until brown and caramelized, 10–12 minutes. Add mushrooms and garlic and cook, stirring occasionally, until mushrooms are soft, about 10 minutes; remove from heat and set aside

3 ◆ In a small bowl, stir together the goat cheese, milk and Parmesan until smooth. Stir the cheese sauce into the cooked pasta; fold in the mushroom mixture and half of the chives. Garnish with additional chives and pepper to taste.

✕◆✕ Spaghetti and Parmesan with Fried Egg

This dish is all about comfort food—like the macaroni and butter you enjoyed as a kid, but all grown up. Ⓓ **Serves 4**

1 pound spaghetti (regular or whole wheat)
2 tablespoons olive oil
4 large eggs
4 tablespoons unsalted butter, melted

Salt and freshly ground black pepper
1/2 cup chopped flat-leaf parsley
1 teaspoon dried thyme
1 cup grated Parmesan cheese, plus additional for sprinkling

1 ◆ Cook spaghetti according to package directions until al dente; drain and set aside.

2 ◆ Meanwhile, heat oil in a large nonstick pan over medium-low heat. Crack eggs into the pan one at a time, gently nudging the yolks toward the center of the whites with a spoon. (The whites will probably run all around the pan, but this is pure comfort food, so looks don't matter!)

3 ◆ Allow eggs to cook until whites begin to crinkle around the edges, 4–6 minutes; flip, turn off heat and let cook for another minute until whites are set and yolks are still a bit runny (or longer, if you prefer cooked yolks).

4 ◆ Transfer spaghetti to a large bowl; add butter, salt and pepper to taste, parsley, thyme and Parmesan and toss with a pair of tongs to fully coat the spaghetti. Divide between four bowls; top each bowl with an egg, a little extra Parmesan and more pepper.

VARIATIONS: Change up this dish by topping it with poached eggs instead of fried and adding a sautéed green like broccoli rabe to the mix.

SWEETS

·······◈◆◈·······

Sweets

Jewish tradition knows how to please a sweet tooth: Rugelach, cheesecake, sufganiyot (donuts), hamantashen, babka. These love and labor-intensive desserts have helped to enhance many holiday tables and bring extra joy to countless *simcha*s. But when it comes to everyday desserts—the cookie after school to tide the kids over until dinner, a satisfying nibble of something sweet after a meal or a late-night ice cream craving—simplicity is key.

◆ ◆ ◆

Then there is the health factor. On the one hand, a good dessert satisfies a certain primal desire for decadence that a fat-free pudding cup just can't match. But indulging in super-rich sweets is not an ideal everyday activity. So stick with small portions of heart-healthy desserts—like fresh fruit or baked goods made with whole wheat flour—most of the time. Then, when the mood strikes for chocolate or whipped cream (or both), choose high-quality ingredients, invite friends over to share and savor every bite.

◆ ◆ ◆

Several of the desserts in this section, like the **Grilled Pineapple with Minted Raspberry Smash** *(page 191)* and **Coconut Tapioca Pudding** *(page 186)*, are naturally pareve, making them the perfect follow-up to a meat meal. Others, like the no-bake **Raspberry Cheesecake in a Jar** *(page 183)*, **Cinnamon-Chocolate Pudding** *(page 185)* and **Ginger Ice Cream Sandwiches** *(page 176)*, are unabashedly dairy. Serve these treats after vegetarian or fish meals when you can enjoy them to their fullest.

◆ ◆ ◆

The third category of desserts—like the **Maple Baked Pears** *(page 192)* and **Chocolate Pomegranate Gushers** *(page 187)*—can easily swing in either the dairy or pareve direction. When going pareve, avoid nondairy creamers and whipped toppings, which are typically loaded with unhealthy additives and preservatives. Instead, use non-hydrogenated margarine and soy, almond, rice or coconut milk alternatives, which are readily available in most supermarkets and deliver good flavor.

◆ ◆ ◆

What connects all of these desserts is that they come together without a lot of fuss. So save the crème brulée for a night out and the apple strudel for Rosh Hashana, and enjoy dessert everyday-style instead.

PAGES **170–171**: *Glazed Cinnamon Oatmeal Cookies, recipe, page 175*

Almond Butter Chocolate Chip Cookies

Try these nutty, chocolate-studded beauties when you are craving an alternative to regular peanut butter chocolate chip cookies. Ⓓ **Makes about two dozen cookies**

1 cup all-purpose flour
3/4 cup whole wheat flour
3/4 teaspoon baking powder
1/2 teaspoon salt
1/2 cup unsalted butter, softened
3/4 cup packed brown sugar

1 large egg
3 tablespoons milk
1/2 teaspoon vanilla extract
1/2 cup almond butter
3/4 cup milk chocolate chips

1 ◆ Preheat oven to 375 degrees. In a small bowl, combine flours, baking powder and salt; set aside.

2 ◆ In a large bowl or standing mixer, cream the butter and sugar together until fluffy, 3–4 minutes. Add the egg, milk and vanilla and cream until smooth. Stir in the almond butter, then incorporate the dry mixture into the wet until combined. Fold in the chocolate chips.

3 ◆ Drop heaping teaspoons of dough onto an ungreased cookie sheet. Bake until lightly browned, about 10 minutes. Transfer to a wire rack to cool.

Mocha Shortbread

These flaky, buttery cookies have all the breezy charm of an outdoor café and taste wonderful with a steaming cup of tea or coffee. Ⓓ Ⓟ **Makes about 2 dozen cookies**

1 cup unsalted butter or non-
    hydrogenated margarine,
    softened
2/3 cup confectioners' sugar
2 teaspoons vanilla extract

2 cups all-purpose flour
1/4 cup cocoa powder
2 teaspoons instant espresso powder
    or instant coffee powder
1/2 teaspoon salt

1 ◆ Preheat oven to 300 degrees. In a small bowl, stir together flour, cocoa powder, espresso and salt; set aside.

2 ◆ Beat butter and sugar together until creamy using a wooden spoon or electric mixer. Add vanilla and beat well to incorporate. Add dry mixture to wet and combine.

3 ◆ Using your fingers, press dough evenly into the bottom of a lightly

greased 9 x 13-inch pan. (Dip your fingers in a bit of flour if they are sticking to the dough.) Prick the shortbread in several places with a fork and, using a sharp knife, cut it into rectangles (but do not lift pieces out of pan).

4 ◆ Bake for 15–20 minutes until shortbread is set. Remove from oven and, while still hot, cut shortbread along original scoring lines. Allow pan to cool on a wire rack before removing cookies from pan.

⋈◆⋊ Glazed Cinnamon Oatmeal Cookies

Whole oats and dried fruit add to these cookies' nutritional profile. The sweet cinnamon glaze is optional, but turns them into a real treat. Ⓓ Ⓟ **Makes about 2 dozen cookies**

FOR COOKIES:
1/2 cup unsalted butter or
    non-hydrogenated
    margarine, softened
1 cup packed brown sugar
1 large egg
1 teaspoon vanilla extract
1/2 teaspoon lemon zest
1 1/4 cups all-purpose flour
1/2 teaspoon baking soda
1/2 teaspoon salt
1 teaspoon cinnamon

2 cups rolled oats (not instant)
1/2 cup dried cranberries or
    raisins
1/2 cup pecans, chopped (optional)

FOR GLAZE:
1 cup confectioners' sugar
1/2 teaspoon vanilla extract
1/2 teaspoon cinnamon
2 tablespoons milk (or dairy-free
    substitute like soy or almond
    milk)

1 ◆ Preheat oven to 350 degrees. In a medium bowl, stir together the flour, baking soda, salt and cinnamon; set aside.

2 ◆ In a standing mixer or by hand with a wooden spoon, beat the butter and sugar together until creamy, 2–3 minutes. Add the egg, vanilla and lemon zest and mix well to combine.

3 ◆ Add the dry mixture to the creamed mixture and mix until incorporated. Fold in the oats, cranberries or raisins and pecans, if using.

4 ◆ Drop mounds of batter (about 1 teaspoon) onto an ungreased baking sheet approximately 2 inches apart. Using your hand or the back of a spoon, flatten the cookies slightly. Bake for 12–15 minutes until lightly golden around the edges, but still slightly soft in the center. Remove from oven; let cool for a few minutes on the baking sheet, then transfer to a wire rack to cool completely before glazing.

5 ◆ To make the glaze, combine all ingredients in a small bowl and whisk vigorously until smooth. Drizzle on top of cookies once they cool.

NON-HYDROGENATED MARGARINE

◆ ◆ ◆ ◆ ◆

For years, margarine was touted as the healthier alternative to butter. But many margarine brands are filled with unhealthy hydrogenated oils and trans fats, which actually contribute to heart disease and high cholesterol.

In recent years, several margarine brands emerged that replaced the hydrogenated ingredients with heart-healthy oils. When cooking or baking pareve dishes, look for margarines that say non-hydrogenated and trans-fat free on the package.

Glazed Cinnamon Oatmeal Cookies, photo pages 170–171

❦◆❧ Ginger Ice Cream Sandwiches

Spicy, sweet and creamy—this ice cream sandwich has it all. If you do not have time to assemble the sandwiches, simply spoon the ice cream into a bowl and top with a cookie. Ⓓ **Makes about 2 1/2 dozen cookies or 15 sandwiches**

2 1/4 cups all-purpose flour	3/4 cup unsalted butter, softened
2 teaspoons baking soda	1 cup packed brown sugar
2 teaspoons ginger powder	1 large egg
1 teaspoon cinnamon	1/4 cup molasses
1/4 teaspoon allspice	3 tablespoons grated fresh ginger
Pinch of nutmeg	Half gallon vanilla ice cream, very
1/2 teaspoon salt	slightly softened

1 ◆ Preheat oven to 350 degrees. In a medium bowl, stir together flour, baking soda, ginger powder, cinnamon, allspice, nutmeg and salt; set aside.

2 ◆ In a large bowl or standing mixer, cream together the butter and brown sugar until smooth. Mix in the egg, molasses and ginger. Gradually add dry mixture to wet and mix until fully incorporated.

3 ◆ Chill dough until it reaches rolling consistency, 12–15 minutes; roll dough into 1-inch balls and place on an ungreased cookie sheet about 2 inches apart. Using a spatula or your palm, flatten the cookies slightly. Bake until set, 8–10 minutes. (Keep any unrolled dough in the refrigerator while cookies are baking.) Cool completely on wire racks.

4 ◆ *Assemble sandwiches:* Spoon approximately 4 tablespoons ice cream on one cookie. Top with second cookie and press lightly to flatten. Place sandwich on a cookie sheet and store in freezer while assembling other sandwiches.

Ginger Ice Cream Sandwiches ▶

⊀◆⊱ Olive Oil Cookies

Using olive oil instead of butter or margarine in these cookies is a healthy surprise. Use a good quality extra-virgin olive oil, which helps the cookies spread nicely but still maintain an airy structure.
Ⓓ Ⓟ **Makes about 2 1/2 dozen cookies**

1 3/4 cups flour
1 1/4 cups sugar
1/4 teaspoon baking powder
1/8 teaspoon salt
1/2 cup extra-virgin olive oil
1/3 cup milk (or dairy-free substitute like soy or almond milk)

1 large egg
1 teaspoon vanilla extract
2 teaspoons lemon zest
2 teaspoons sesame seeds or anise seeds (optional)

1 ◆ Preheat oven to 350 degrees. Line cookie sheets with parchment paper and set aside.

2 ◆ Mix together flour, sugar, baking powder and salt in a large bowl. In a separate bowl, whisk together oil, milk, egg, vanilla, lemon zest and sesame or anise seeds, if using.

3 ◆ Add wet ingredients to dry ingredients and stir until just combined; batter will be fairly thick. Drop scant 1 tablespoon of batter onto cookie sheets, letting batter spread slightly and leaving about 2 inches between cookies.

4 ◆ Bake until edges are golden brown, 11–13 minutes. Remove cookies from oven and let cool slightly. Transfer cookies to a wire rack and cool completely. Store in an airtight container for up to 3 days, or freeze in a zip-top bag for up to 1 month.

⊀◆⊱ Orange Chocolate Macaroons

Think macaroons are a Passover-only treat? Studded with bites of chocolate and lightly perfumed with orange, these macaroons come together in minutes and are delightful any time of year.
Ⓓ **Makes 2 1/2 dozen cookies**

2/3 cup sweetened condensed milk
1 egg white
1 1/2 teaspoons vanilla extract
Scant 1/4 teaspoon orange extract

1/8 teaspoon salt
3 1/2 cups shredded unsweetened coconut
1/2 cup semisweet chocolate chips

1 ◆ Preheat oven to 325 degrees. Line a baking sheet with parchment paper and set aside.

2 ◆ Whisk the condensed milk, egg white, vanilla, orange extract and salt in a medium bowl until well combined. Fold in the coconut, followed by the chocolate chips.

3 ◆ Drop tablespoonfuls of batter onto the baking sheet. Bake until cookies are lightly browned, 20–25 minutes. Cool slightly, then peel cookies from the parchment. Store leftovers in an airtight container.

❈◆❈ Lemon Lime Squares

The combination of lemon and lime juices in these custard-topped shortbread bars results in perfect mouth-puckering flavor. Ⓓ Ⓟ **Makes 16 squares**

FOR SHORTBREAD:
1 cup all-purpose flour
1/4 cup confectioners' sugar, plus
*   more for dusting*
1/4 teaspoon salt
1/2 cup plus 2 tablespoons
*   cold unsalted butter or non-*
*   hydrogenated margarine, cut*
*   into pieces*

FOR TOPPING:
1 teaspoon lemon zest
1 teaspoon lime zest
1/4 cup fresh lemon juice
1/4 cup fresh lime juice
4 large eggs
1 cup sugar
1/4 cup all-purpose flour
1/2 teaspoon salt

1 ◆ Preheat oven to 350 degrees. Lightly grease an 8 x 8-inch pan. Add flour, sugar, salt and butter or margarine to a food processor and pulse until the mixture resembles coarse crumbs. (If you don't have a food processor, you can complete this step in a large bowl using your hands to mix the ingredients.)

2 ◆ Press crumbs evenly into the bottom of the pan; score in several places with a fork and bake until lightly golden, 15–20 minutes. Remove from oven and cool on a wire rack while making the topping.

3 ◆ In a medium bowl, whisk together the lemon and lime zests, lemon and lime juices, eggs and sugar. Add the flour and salt and mix to combine.

4 ◆ Pour topping onto warm crust; bake an additional 15–20 minutes until the top sets. Allow to fully cool, then slice into squares and dust with reserved confectioners' sugar. Store in an airtight container in the refrigerator and dust with fresh confectioners' sugar before serving.

❈◆❈ Brownies with Pomegranate Whipped Cream

These rich, gooey brownies get topped with dollops of sweet-tart, pomegranate-infused whipped cream for a decadent treat.

ⓓ **Makes 12 brownies**

FOR BROWNIES:
3/4 cup all-purpose flour
1/2 cup cocoa powder
1 teaspoon baking powder
1/8 teaspoon salt
3/4 cup unsalted butter, melted
1 1/2 cups sugar
2 large eggs
2 teaspoons vanilla extract

FOR POMEGRANATE WHIPPED CREAM:
1/2 cup heavy whipping cream
1 teaspoon confectioners' sugar
1 tablespoon pomegranate juice
Pomegranate seeds for garnish (optional)

➤**TIP** *If you prefer thicker brownies, pour batter into a greased 8 x 8- or 9 x 9-inch pan and bake for 30–35 minutes, or until a tester inserted in the middle comes out clean.*

1 ◆ Preheat oven to 350 degrees. Grease a 9 x 13-inch baking pan; set aside.

2 ◆ In a medium bowl, whisk together flour, cocoa, baking powder and salt; set aside. In a larger bowl or standing mixer, cream the butter and sugar together until fully combined, about 3 minutes. Add eggs and vanilla, mixing well to combine.

3 ◆ Slowly incorporate dry mixture into wet mixture, mixing gently until just combined (do not over stir). Spread mixture evenly into prepared pan and bake 20–25 minutes, or until a tester inserted in the middle comes out clean. Cool on a wire rack.

4 ◆ *Make the whipped cream:* Whip all ingredients except seeds with cold beaters or immersion blender until soft peaks form, about 30 seconds. Dollop on brownie squares and garnish with pomegranate seeds, if desired.

◀ *Brownies with Pomegranate Whipped Cream*

❊❖❊ Raspberry Cheesecake in a Jar

In *The Book of Jewish Food* (Knopf), Claudia Roden writes that Jews first started making kasekuchen (cheesecake in German) in Central and Eastern Europe in the 18th century. This no-bake riff on original cheesecake layers all of its tastiest components into a glass Mason jar for a whimsical presentation. Ⓓ **Serves 6**

1 1/2 cups graham cracker crumbs (about nine graham cracker sheets)
1/4 cup plus 2 tablespoons sugar, divided
1 teaspoon ginger powder (optional)
6 tablespoons unsalted butter, melted

1 8-ounce package cream cheese, slightly softened
1 1/2 cups ricotta cheese
1 teaspoon lemon zest
1/2 cup heavy cream (or 1 can real whipped cream)
1 jar raspberry preserves
1/4 cup fresh raspberries (optional)

1 ◆ In a medium bowl, combine the graham cracker crumbs, 1 table-spoon sugar, ginger, if desired, and butter; stir well to combine and set aside.

2 ◆ In a large bowl, beat the cream cheese and 1/4 cup sugar together until creamy—either by hand with a wooden spoon or in a standing mixer on low speed. Fold in the ricotta and lemon zest until well combined; set aside.

3 ◆ Using an immersion blender or beaters, whip the heavy cream and 1 tablespoon sugar until peaks form, about 30 seconds. (Omit this step if using store-bought whipped cream.)

4 ◆ *Assemble the cheesecakes:* Divide the graham cracker "crust" into 6 small Mason jars, gently pressing the mixture into the bottom with a spoon or your fingers. (If you do not have Mason jars, small glass cups work just fine.) Top with cheese mixture followed by a dollop of raspberry jam and whipped cream. Sprinkle a few fresh raspberries on top as garnish, if desired.

5 ◆ Serve immediately or chill cheesecake in refrigerator for up to 12 hours; let soften for a few minutes and top with whipped cream just before serving.

◀ *Raspberry Cheesecake in a Jar*

✤✦✤ Moistest Chocolate Cake

With just a hint of coffee mingling with the deep cocoa flavor, this dessert might convince you to never serve a store-bought birthday cake again. ⒟ ⓟ **Makes 1 cake**

FOR CAKE:
2 cups all-purpose flour
1 teaspoon salt
1 teaspoon baking powder
3/4 cup cocoa powder
2 cups sugar
1 cup hot instant coffee
1 cup vegetable oil
1 cup milk (or dairy-free substitute
*   like soy or almond milk)*
1 teaspoon vanilla extract
2 large eggs

FOR FROSTING:
2 cups confectioners' sugar
1 teaspoon unsalted butter or
*   non-hydrogenated margarine,*
*   melted*
1 teaspoon vanilla extract
2–3 tablespoons milk (or dairy-
*   free substitute like soy or*
*   almond milk)*
2 teaspoons cocoa powder
*   (optional)*

1 ◆ Preheat oven to 350 degrees. Grease and lightly flour a 9 x 13-inch pan and set aside.

2 ◆ In a medium bowl or standing mixer, combine flour, salt, baking powder, cocoa powder and sugar. Add coffee, oil and milk and mix by hand with a wooden spoon (or on a low mixer setting) until well combined, about 3 minutes. Add vanilla and eggs, beating well until incorporated.

3 ◆ Pour mixture into the prepared pan and bake 25–30 minutes, or until a tester inserted in the middle comes out clean. Let cool completely before frosting.

4 ◆ *Make the frosting:* In a medium bowl, combine all frosting ingredients and beat together until smooth. If too thick or dry, add more milk, 1 teaspoon at a time. Spread carefully onto cake using an offset spatula. If frosting sticks to spatula, dip it into hot water and proceed.

✤✦✤ Malabi with Pistachios

According to Janna Gur's *The New Book of Israeli Food* (Schocken), malabi originally hails from Turkey. Today, this rose water-perfumed dessert is popular throughout the Middle East, including Israel, where it has become a beloved street snack. ⒟ **Serves 4**

4 cups milk, divided
1/2 cup cornstarch
1 tablespoon rose water

1/2 teaspoon vanilla extract
1/3 cup sugar
Chopped pistachios for garnish

1 ◆ In a medium bowl, mix one cup of milk with the cornstarch, rose water and vanilla until the cornstarch dissolves; set aside.

2 ◆ Bring remaining milk and sugar to a simmer in a saucepan over medium heat, stirring constantly. Lower the heat, pour in the dissolved cornstarch mixture and cook 6–8 minutes, stirring constantly, until the mixture begins to thicken.

3 ◆ Remove mixture from the stove and pour into serving dishes or ramekins. Serve warm topped with chopped pistachios, or cover with plastic wrap and refrigerate for at least 4 hours until fully set and top with chopped pistachios before serving.

✄◆✄ Cinnamon-Chocolate Pudding

Using a blender helps this rich pudding come together quickly—then it's just chill and enjoy. Serve it topped with whipped cream and berries or chocolate shavings. Ⓓ **Serves 4–6**

2 large eggs
1 teaspoon vanilla extract
3 tablespoons cocoa powder
2 tablespoons cornstarch
1 1/2 teaspoons cinnamon

3 tablespoons sugar
4 ounces semisweet chocolate,
*   chopped*
1 cup milk
2/3 cup heavy cream

1 ◆ Add eggs, vanilla, cocoa powder, cornstarch, cinnamon and sugar to blender and process until smooth. Scrape down sides with a rubber spatula. Add chocolate and blend until combined; set aside.

2 ◆ In a small saucepan, heat milk and cream over medium-low heat (not higher), stirring occasionally, until simmering. Immediately pour milk mixture into blender; cover and blend on high until smooth (hold the lid down firmly when blending), stopping to scrape down the sides when necessary.

3 ◆ Pour into 4–6 cups or ramekins (this pudding is very rich and chocolatey, so a little goes a long way). Cover with plastic wrap and chill for 3 hours, until set.

❧◆❧ Coconut Tapioca Pudding

This pudding relies on coconut and almond milk instead of dairy for its silky, creamy texture, making it a perfect ending to a meat meal. **P Makes approximately 4 cups**

1 13 1/2-ounce can coconut milk	1/4 teaspoon salt
1/2 cup small pearl tapioca	2 tablespoons vanilla extract,
2 1/2 cups almond milk	divided
1/4 cup honey	1/4 teaspoon cinnamon (optional)
1/4 cup maple syrup	1/8 teaspoon cardamom (optional)

1 ◆ In a large saucepan, stir together coconut milk and tapioca. Cover and let soak for 15 minutes. Stir in almond milk, honey, maple syrup, salt and 1 tablespoon vanilla.

2 ◆ Bring mixture to a simmer over medium heat, stirring frequently to keep tapioca from sticking to the bottom of the pot. Continue cooking, stirring occasionally, until the mixture starts to thicken and the tapioca becomes translucent, about 15 minutes. Be careful not to overcook or the tapioca will become gluey.

3 ◆ Stir in remaining tablespoon vanilla and the cinnamon or cardamom, if using, and remove from heat. Transfer to a bowl, cover and refrigerate until chilled. Keeps well for up to one week in the refrigerator.

❧◆❧ Orange Floats

Relive a childhood favorite with this creamsicle-inspired dessert. Don't forget your straw! **D Serves 4**

1 pint vanilla ice cream	Seltzer
2 cups orange juice	1 tangerine, peeled and
(not from concentrate)	sectioned
4 tablespoons orange liqueur	
(optional)	

◆ Add one heaping scoop of ice cream to each of four medium glasses. Add half a cup of orange juice to each. (If using the liqueur, stir it into the orange juice before adding to the glasses). Top off each glass with about 1/2 cup of seltzer and garnish with one or two sections of tangerine.

⊹◆⊱ Strawberries and Cream with Toasted Hazelnuts

Light, sweet and sumptuous, this dessert delivers on all fronts. The sugar in this recipe will coax flavor from any strawberry, but for truly over-the-top taste, wait until in-season strawberries show up at the farmers' market. Ⓓ **Serves 6**

2 pints fresh strawberries, stemmed and sliced	*1 cup heavy cream*
Juice of 1/2 a lemon	*1 cup hazelnuts, toasted and chopped*
3 tablespoons sugar, divided	

1 ◆ Combine the strawberries, lemon juice and 2 tablespoons sugar in a medium bowl, stir gently and set aside.

2 ◆ Pour whipping cream in a deep bowl. Add remaining tablespoon of sugar and stir gently to combine. Using an immersion blender or cold beaters, whip the cream until soft peaks form, about 30 seconds to 1 minute.

3 ◆ Divide strawberries into individual bowls. Top with whipped cream and sprinkle with hazelnuts. Serve immediately.

⊹◆⊱ Chocolate Pomegranate Gushers

Using dark chocolate for this recipe adds a pleasing, bitter complement to the sweet juiciness of pomegranate seeds, but feel free to substitute milk chocolate if you prefer. Ⓓ Ⓟ **Makes about 2 dozen gushers**

1 1/2 cups pomegranate seeds	*1 pound dark chocolate*

1 ◆ Line a cookie sheet with wax paper and set aside. Melt chocolate in a double boiler or stainless steel bowl set over simmering water, stirring frequently until melted, 3–5 minutes. (Or place chocolate in a microwave-safe bowl and microwave, stirring every 30 seconds, until melted.)

2 ◆ Remove chocolate from heat and add pomegranate seeds, stirring thoroughly to coat while being careful not to pop any seeds. Use a spoon or small ice-cream scoop to drop mounds of chocolate-covered seeds onto wax paper. Refrigerate for at least one hour or until chocolate sets.

REMOVING POMEGRANATE SEEDS

◆◆◆◆◆

Pomegranates add gorgeous color and tangy sweetness to recipes, but removing the jewel-like seeds can be a messy endeavor—unless you follow this simple method: Cut the pomegranate into quarters. Fill a bowl halfway with water; dunk the pomegranate quarters in the water and, using your fingers, remove the seeds from the peel and white membranes. The seeds sink to the bottom while the peel floats to the top. When you finish removing the seeds, skim off the membranes, then pour the water and seeds through a sieve. You will be left with beautiful, ready-to-use seeds.

✦✦ Year-Round Fruit Crumble

Crumbles are one of the easiest and most satisfying desserts to make. A good crumble topping tastes delicious on just about any combination of fruit, which means one recipe can take you through the whole year, changing as new fruits come into season. Make a double (or even triple) batch of the topping and freeze the excess, so it's ready whenever the crumble craving strikes.

Ⓓ Ⓟ Serves 6

CRUMBLE TOPPING:
1/2 cup all-purpose flour
3/4 cup rolled oats (not instant)
1/4 cup packed brown sugar
1/2 teaspoon cinnamon
1/2 teaspoon ginger powder (optional)

Pinch of salt
7 tablespoons cold, unsalted butter or non-hydrogenated margarine, cut into small pieces

1 ◆ Stir to combine the dry ingredients in a medium bowl. Add the butter or margarine and, using your fingers or a food processor, incorporate the ingredients until the mixture resembles coarse crumbs.

2 ◆ Preheat oven to 375 degrees. Sprinkle topping liberally over an 8 x 8-inch glass dish filled with fruit mixture. Bake until topping is golden brown and fruit is bubbling, 25–30 minutes. Serve with fresh whipped cream or vanilla or cinnamon ice cream after a dairy meal.

❊ WINTER CRUMBLE
PEAR AND CHOCOLATE: Combine 4–5 ripe pears cut into 1/4-inch pieces with juice of 1/2 a lemon and 1/4 cup sugar. Add 2/3 cup semisweet chocolate chips to crumble topping.

❊ SPRING CRUMBLE
STRAWBERRY RHUBARB: Combine 1 1/2 pounds trimmed and sliced rhubarb with 1/2 cup sliced strawberries, 1/4 cup sugar and 1 teaspoon orange zest and simmer until slightly softened, about 5–7 minutes.

❊ SUMMER CRUMBLE
STONE FRUIT: Pit and slice 2 pounds of any of the following fruits (or any combination thereof): apricots, peaches, nectarines or plums. Combine with 1/3 cup sugar and two tablespoons cornstarch.

❊ FALL CRUMBLE
APPLE CRANBERRY: Combine 4 baking apples (like Cortland, Mutsu or Empire) cored and cut into 1-inch pieces with 1 cup fresh or thawed frozen cranberries, juice of 1/2 a lemon and 1/3 cup sugar.

RECONSTITUTING BROWN SUGAR
✦✦✦✦✦

Virtually every home cook has opened a box of brown sugar to find a dried out, disappointing lump staring back at them. While the sugar is essentially useless in this state, it is easy to revive.

Place sugar in a Tupperware or other container with a tight-fitting lid. Add one whole piece of bread (any type will do), cover and let sit for 24 hours. The bread's moisture transfers to the sugar, making it soft and pliable again. Don't have a whole day? Place the sugar in a microwave-safe container with the bread on top. Cover and microwave for 15 seconds.

Stone Fruit Crumble: ▶

Grilled Pineapple with Minted Raspberry Smash

Serve this luscious, fruity dessert as the grand finale to a summer backyard barbecue party. **ⓟ Serves 4–6**

FOR PINEAPPLE:
1 whole pineapple
1/2 cup packed brown sugar
   dissolved in a little water
1 tablespoon fresh lime juice

FOR SMASH:
1 cup fresh raspberries (do not
   use frozen)
1 tablespoon sugar
1 tablespoon fresh mint, chopped

1 ◆ Using a sharp, sturdy knife, cut the bottom off of the pineapple. Stand the pineapple up on a flat surface and, slicing down along the fruit, remove the outer peel, rotating as you go until the peel is gone. Lay the pineapple down horizontally and slice into 1/2-inch rounds or cut into 1/2-inch long wedges.

2 ◆ Mix together the dissolved brown sugar and lime juice in a small bowl. Using a pastry brush, lightly coat each pineapple round or wedge with the mixture. Spray your grill or a grill pan with a little vegetable oil and grill pineapple on each side for a couple of minutes until it is nicely caramelized and browned.

3 ◆ *Make the smash:* Combine raspberries, sugar and mint in a medium bowl. Using a fork, smash the raspberries and other ingredients together. Allow to sit for at least 10 minutes before dolloping onto grilled pineapple.

◀ *Grilled Pineapple with Minted Raspberry Smash*

✖◆✖ Maple Baked Pears

Sweetened with maple syrup and softened with dots of butter, this dish rivals baked apples as autumn's coziest dessert. **D** **P** **Serves 4**

✦TIP *For the best flavor in this dish, make sure to use 100 pure percent maple syrup.*

4 ripe Bartlett pears, cored and quartered
3 tablespoons unsalted butter or non-hydrogenated margarine, cut into pieces

1/4 cup pure maple syrup
1 teaspoon vanilla extract
1/2 teaspoon cinnamon
1 teaspoon bourbon (optional)

◆ Preheat oven to 450 degrees. Arrange pears in a baking dish and dot with butter or margarine. In a small bowl, combine maple syrup, vanilla, cinnamon and bourbon, if using; drizzle over pears. Bake for 15–20 minutes, until soft and caramelized.

✖◆✖ Broiled Grapefruit with Brown Sugar

A flash of heat softens and sweetens brown sugar-topped grapefruit, leaving it slightly caramelized and incredibly juicy. **P** **Serves 4**

2 grapefruits, halved horizontally, seeds removed
4 tablespoons brown sugar

Pinch of cardamom or cinnamon (optional)

1 ◆ Preheat broiler. Section the grapefruit with a sharp knife, cutting around the outside edge and at the seams of each section to loosen them.

2 ◆ Place the grapefruit halves in a baking dish (you can trim a little peel off the bottom to help them sit still without rocking). Spread 1 tablespoon brown sugar onto each half and sprinkle with spices, if using. Broil until sugar is bubbly and fruit is gently warmed through, about 5 minutes.

Sweet Citrus Fruit Salad with Honey and Pistachios

The citrus burst in this dessert salad is mellowed by the addition of rich dates and a sprinkle of pistachio nuts. ℗ **Serves 10–12**

2 large oranges
2 red grapefruits
6 dried dates (preferably Medjool), pitted and chopped
1 1/2 cups seedless grapes (mixture of red and green), halved

1 pomegranate, seeded
1/3 cup coarsely chopped pistachios
3 tablespoons honey

1 ◆ Peel oranges and grapefruits. Thinly slice oranges crosswise and section the grapefruit. Arrange fruit on a large serving platter.

2 ◆ Scatter chopped dates, grapes, and pomegranate seeds over top of citrus fruits. Cover, chill and drizzle with honey and sprinkle with pistachios just before serving.

❈◆❈ Watermelon Ice Pops

These refreshing ice pops get you in and out of the kitchen in minutes and keep you cool on a steamy summer day. If you prefer, pour the blended juice into a pitcher and mix with cold water to taste for a not-too-sweet, refreshing drink. ℗ **Makes 10–15 ice pops**

7 cups seedless watermelon, cubed (about half a medium-sized melon)	*Juice of 1 lime* *2 tablespoons sugar* *1/4 cup orange juice (optional)*

- Purée watermelon, lime juice, sugar and orange juice, if using, in a blender until smooth, 15–30 seconds. Pour juice into ice pop molds and freeze. (Ice cube trays can be used in a pinch.) If desired, strain mixture through a sieve before pouring into molds.

❈◆❈ Rhubarb Sauce

➤**TIP** *Older rhubarb tends to be stringy, like celery. Make sure to pull the strings off before using.*

Eat this hot pink sauce alone or spoon it over ice cream, pound cake, waffles, yogurt—anything that could benefit from a kick of fruity sweetness. ℗ **Makes about 2 cups**

2 cups rhubarb, trimmed and cut into 1/2-inch pieces (approximately 6 stalks)	*1/2 cup sugar* *1 teaspoon orange zest* *1/4 cup water*

- In a small saucepan, combine the rhubarb, sugar, orange zest and water. Cook over low heat, stirring occasionally, until rhubarb is tender and falling apart, 12–15 minutes.

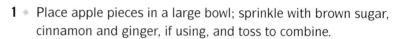

Slow Cooker Applesauce

Apple picking is a popular activity in autumn, but what do you do with your bounty? Make a batch or two of this super simple applesauce and freeze it to enjoy with your latkes all winter long. **℗ Makes 4–5 cups**

10 medium-sized apples
(Gala, Granny Smith, Fuji or
McIntosh), peeled, cored and
sliced into 1/4-inch pieces
1/4 cup packed brown sugar

1 teaspoon cinnamon
1 teaspoon ginger powder
(optional)
1/4 cup water

1 ◆ Place apple pieces in a large bowl; sprinkle with brown sugar, cinnamon and ginger, if using, and toss to combine.

2 ◆ Pour water into the bottom of a large slow cooker and add apple mixture. Cover and set slow cooker to low and cook for 8 hours, stirring occasionally. Serve at room temperature or cover and refrigerate.

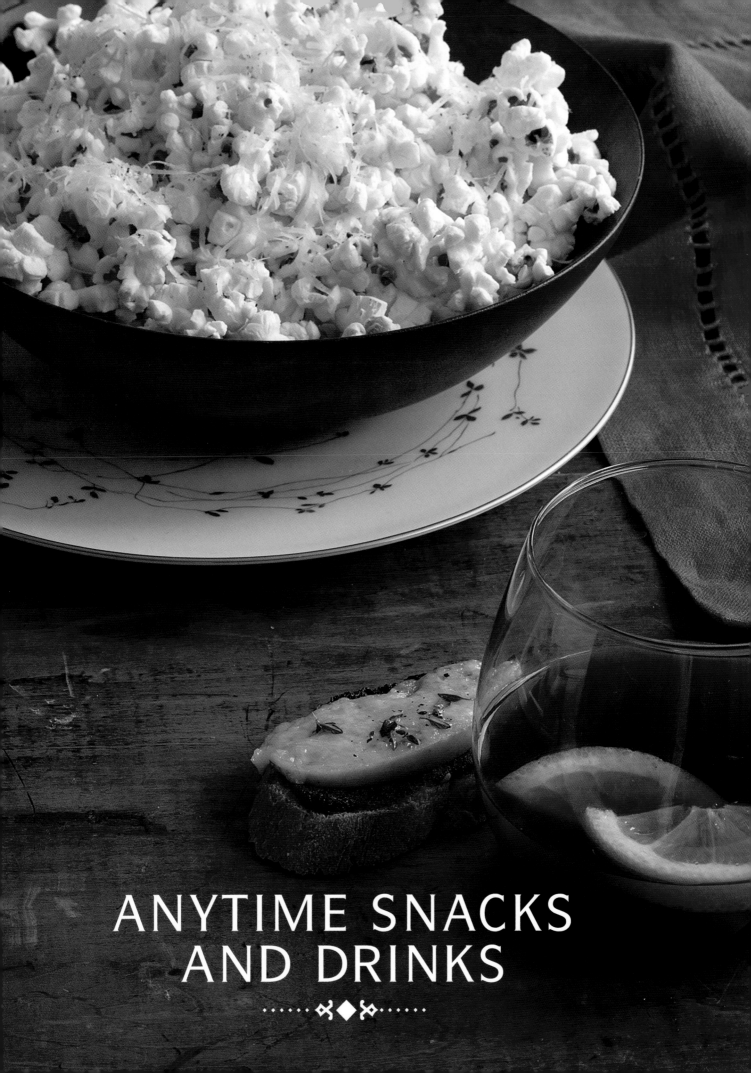

ANYTIME SNACKS
AND DRINKS
⬩⬩⬩⬩⬩⬩ ❖◆❖ ⬩⬩⬩⬩⬩⬩

Anytime Snacks and Drinks

The world is filled with snacks. Blinking vending machines and well-stocked candy bowls beckon at the office. Chocolate bars call out from the impulse-buy racks at the supermarket. Even our own cupboards, stocked with their bags of chips and granola bars, offer forth a never-ending stream of snacking opportunities. Still, the art of good snacking remains elusive.

◆ ◆ ◆

The great 12th-century Jewish sage and physician, Moses Maimonides, promoted the value of moderation in both eating and life. Unfortunately, snacks—those quickly gobbled pseudo-meals eaten to quell mid-morning hunger pangs and afternoon slumps—often ruin our best intentions. How can we be expected to make smart food choices, after all, while running from meeting to meeting? It's so much easier to just grab the nearest prepackaged crunchy (or chewy, sweet or creamy) treat and keep moving.

◆ ◆ ◆

This section aims to reclaim the snack's proper dignity. There is nothing wrong with a little nibble between meals, as long as it is done with care. At the office, a thoughtfully stocked mini-refrigerator and desk drawer is your greatest ally. Spread peanut butter onto a graham cracker and top it with half a sliced banana. Dress up a piece of toast with mustard, pickles and sliced turkey, top a hardboiled egg with salsa or pour a small bowl of granola topped with blueberries and low-fat milk.

◆ ◆ ◆

Back at home, where you have a few more ingredients and cooking appliances at your disposal, whip up some **Crispy Roasted Chickpeas** *(page 200)* and homemade **Parmesan Popcorn** *(page 201)* to crunch on while curling up in front of a movie, or make **Souped-Up Deviled Eggs** *(page 203)* and **Ricotta and Pistachio Stuffed Figs** *(page 206)* to delight guests at your next party.

◆ ◆ ◆

Want something a little heartier? Try the **Broccoli Black Bean Nachos** *(page 204)* to share with friends or family—and don't forget the drinks. From the citrus-packed **Sunshine Sangria** *(page 209)* to the fragrant **Chai Hot Chocolate** *(page 211)*, your anytime snacking needs are covered.

PAGES 196–197: *Rum and Ginger Cocktail, recipe, page 208; Apple Butter Cheddar Toasts, recipe, page 201; Parmesan Popcorn, recipe, page 201; Sunshine Sangria, recipe, page 209*

⋇◆⋇ Harvest Apple Salsa

This refreshing apple salsa pays homage to the last golden days of summer while ushering in the unmistakable crunch of autumn. Serve with corn chips. Ⓟ **Serves 4**

2 apples (red or green), peeled, cored and chopped
1 small to medium onion, roughly chopped
1/2 jalapeño pepper, seeded and finely chopped

2 tablespoons finely chopped cilantro
Juice of 1 lemon
2 teaspoons honey or agave nectar

♦ Combine all ingredients in a medium bowl and stir to combine. Serve immediately or let sit for 15 minutes before serving to allow the flavors to mingle.

⋇◆⋇ Crispy Roasted Chickpeas

Hummus and falafel are not the humble chickpea's only destiny. These crunchy little snacks are easy to make and highly addictive. Roasted chickpeas also make a tasty alternative to salad croutons. Ⓟ **Makes approximately 2 cups**

1 15-ounce can chickpeas, rinsed, drained and thoroughly dried
1 tablespoon olive oil
1/2 teaspoon salt

Any of the following spices (optional): smoked paprika, chili powder, dried thyme and lemon zest, herbes de Provence, garlic powder, cinnamon and sugar, za'atar, cumin, garam masala

1 ♦ Preheat oven to 400 degrees. Stir chickpeas together with oil, salt and desired spices to taste in a medium bowl.

2 ♦ Spread chickpeas on a baking sheet and roast for 30–40 minutes, stirring twice during cooking time, until browned and crunchy.

3 ♦ Transfer baking sheet to a wire rack to cool. If desired, sprinkle with additional salt to taste. The chickpeas taste best eaten fresh, but leftovers can be stored overnight in an airtight container.

❖◆❖ Parmesan Popcorn

▲ *Parmesan Popcorn*

Say goodbye to microwave popcorn and hello to piping hot, Parmesan-spiked popcorn that comes together in 10 minutes or less. ⑩ **Serves 4**

3 tablespoons vegetable oil
1/2 cup popcorn kernels
2 tablespoons unsalted butter, melted

1/4 cup Parmesan cheese, grated
Sea salt

1 ◆ Pour oil into a medium pot set over medium-low heat. Add one popcorn kernel and cover with a tight lid. When the kernel pops (you will hear it hit the underside of the cover), pour in the rest of the kernels, re-cover and cook, shaking the pot occasionally to spread oil around until you hear the kernels stop popping, 5–7 minutes.

2 ◆ Turn off heat and transfer popcorn to a large bowl. Drizzle butter over popcorn and sprinkle on Parmesan and salt to taste, tossing with your fingers to coat popcorn evenly.

❖◆❖ Apple Butter Cheddar Toasts

This dish plays on a classic New England culinary pairing: apple pie and cheddar cheese. A thin layer of apple butter adds an extra sweetness to these toasty hors d'oeuvres. ⑩ **Serves 4–6**

1 baguette sliced into 1/2-inch thick diagonal rounds
1/4–1/2 cup apple butter
2 Granny Smith apples, cored and thinly sliced

1/2 pound sharp white cheddar, thinly sliced
Fresh thyme leaves
Freshly ground black pepper

1 ◆ Preheat broiler. Arrange bread rounds on a baking sheet. Spread each round with a thin layer of apple butter and top with 1–2 apple slices followed by 1–2 cheddar slices (depending on desired thickness).

2 ◆ Broil sandwiches until cheese is melted and lightly browned, 5–7 minutes. Remove from oven and sprinkle with thyme and pepper to taste.

Apple Butter Cheddar Toasts, photo pages 196–197

✕◆✕ Souped-Up Deviled Eggs

If you can make egg salad, you can make deviled eggs. This basic recipe comes with plenty of mix-in options to transform a classic party dish into something to really celebrate. **D** **P** **Serves 4–6**

12 large eggs
4 tablespoons mayonnaise
2 teaspoons mustard
Salt and freshly ground
*   black pepper*
Paprika (for dusting)

Mix-ins (optional): pesto, chopped
*   roasted red pepper, horseradish,*
*   shredded Parmesan or Pecorino*
*   cheese, chives, herbed breadcrumbs,*
*   cayenne powder*

1 ◆ Place eggs in a large saucepan and cover with water. Bring to a boil; turn off heat, cover and let stand for 15 minutes. Remove eggs from water and cool in the refrigerator.

2 ◆ Peel eggs and slice in half lengthwise. Scoop out yolks and place in a small bowl; arrange whites on a platter.

3 ◆ To the egg yolks, add mayonnaise, mustard, salt and pepper to taste and any desired mix-ins, then mash together with a fork until smooth.

4 ◆ Scoop egg-yolk filling into a plastic zip-top bag; snip off a bottom corner of bag and pipe yolk mixture into egg white halves, filling holes completely. Sprinkle paprika on top; refrigerate before serving.

◀ *Souped-Up Deviled Eggs*

❈❖❈ Homemade Pita Chips with Curry Yogurt Dip

Homemade pita chips are almost embarrassingly easy to make. Tell your guests you are serving them this quick and spicy curry dip with "freshly made pita chips" and bask in the culinary admiration. Ⓓ **Serves 6–8**

▲ *Homemade Pita Chips*

FOR PITA CHIPS:
3 whole pitas
3 tablespoons olive oil
Sea salt and freshly
*   ground black pepper*

FOR YOGURT DIP:
1 cup Greek yogurt (or plain yogurt)
1/2 teaspoon curry powder
1/4 teaspoon garlic powder
1/4 teaspoon cayenne powder
Salt

1 ◆ *Make the pita chips:* Preheat oven to 400 degrees. Brush pitas with oil and sprinkle with sea salt and pepper to taste. Slice each pita into 8 wedges; arrange in one layer on a baking sheet. Bake until crispy and browned, 8–10 minutes.

2 ◆ While pita chips are cooking, make the yogurt dip: Place all ingredients in a small bowl and mix well to combine. Adjust seasonings according to taste.

❈❖❈ Broccoli Black Bean Nachos

These nachos are a great accompaniment for game day, your monthly mahjong club or a stay-at-home movie night. The nutritious addition of sautéed broccoli and black beans transforms this snack into a virtual meal. Play around with toppings (swap sautéed kale for the broccoli, or use kidney beans instead of black beans) until you find a combination you love. Ⓓ **Serves 6**

2 tablespoons olive oil
1/2 head broccoli, washed and
cut into small florets
1 8-ounce bag corn chips (blue or
yellow)
1 15-ounce can black beans,
rinsed and drained

1/2 teaspoon garlic powder
1/2 teaspoon dried basil
1 1/2 cups shredded cheddar
cheese
Suggested toppings: salsa,
chopped scallions, avocado
slices, sour cream

1 ◆ Preheat oven to 375 degrees. Heat oil in a large pan over medium heat. Add broccoli, cover and cook until florets are slightly wilted but still bright green, about 5 minutes; remove from heat.

2 ◆ Spread half of the corn chips evenly on a rimmed baking sheet. Top with broccoli, black beans, garlic powder, basil and half of the cheese. Spread the second half of the corn chips on top, followed by the remaining cheese.

3 ◆ Bake in oven until cheese is melted and slightly browned, 12–15 minutes. Finish with desired toppings.

⊶◆⊷ Roasted Garlic and Tomato Bruschetta

Rich, velvety roasted garlic and fresh tomato pair perfectly in this satisfying hors d'oeuvre. ℗ **Serves 6**

1 head garlic
2 tablespoons olive oil, divided
3 medium ripe tomatoes (heirloom
or beefsteak), seeded and
chopped
3 tablespoons chopped basil

1/4 teaspoon red pepper flakes
1 baguette sliced into 1/4-inch
pieces, lightly toasted
Sea salt and freshly ground black
pepper

1 ◆ Preheat oven to 400 degrees. Slice off the top of the garlic head, exposing the tops of the cloves. Place on aluminum foil, drizzle with 1 tablespoon oil and wrap lightly; bake for 30 minutes. Remove garlic from oven and cool; squeeze the cloves out of their shells into a small bowl and set aside.

2 ◆ Meanwhile, combine tomato, basil, red pepper flakes and remaining tablespoon of oil in a small bowl. Add in roasted garlic and gently mash with rest of ingredients until combined. Spread a heaping tablespoon of the mixture onto each baguette slice and sprinkle with salt and pepper to taste.

�֍◆֍ Ricotta and Pistachio-Stuffed Figs

This decadent but healthy snack pairs fresh figs with luscious ricotta cheese and crunchy pistachio crumbs. They work equally well as dessert. ⓓ **Serves 4–6**

8 fresh figs, split down the middle (but not cut all the way through)

1/2 cup ricotta cheese

1/4 cup shelled pistachios, finely chopped

4 tablespoons honey or agave nectar

4 tablespoons mint, finely chopped

◆ Fill the split of each fig with a generous dollop of ricotta. Dip stuffed end into chopped pistachios; arrange on a large plate or serving platter. Once all figs have been stuffed, drizzle with honey and sprinkle with fresh mint.

SERVING VARIATION: After stuffing a fig with ricotta, dip the un-cut, rounded-bottom end into a little honey followed by the pistachios, then proceed with instructions (in photo, opposite page).

✖◆✖ Pomegranate Mimosa

Adding this antioxidant-rich fruit juice lends a Mediterranean accent to the classic brunch drink ⓟ **Serves 8**

2 cups pomegranate juice

1 cup fresh orange juice

1 bottle champagne or sparkling wine

Pomegranate seeds for garnish (optional)

◆ Whisk pomegranate juice and orange juice together in a large pitcher; slowly add champagne and stir to combine. Pour drink into champagne flutes and toss in a few fresh pomegranate seeds, if desired.

Ricotta and Pistachio-Stuffed Figs ▶

*Rum and Ginger Cocktail,
photo page 196*

❖❖❖ Rum and Ginger Cocktail

This take on the Dark 'N' Stormy adds a ginger-sugared rim for an extra sweet-spicy kick. Ⓟ **Serves 4**

1/2 cup sugar
1 teaspoon ginger powder
1 lime, quartered

5 ounces dark rum
4 12-ounce bottles of ginger beer (not ginger ale)

1 ◆ Stir together sugar and ginger powder in a shallow bowl. Run a lime wedge around the edge of four highball glasses, then dip each glass in the sugar and ginger mixture.

2 ◆ Add 2–3 ice cubes followed by 1 1/4 ounces rum to each glass. Pour in ginger beer, stir and serve garnished with lime wedge.

⋉◆⋊ Sunshine Sangria

This sangria gets a boost of sunny flavor from three different citrus fruits. ℗ **Serves 4**

2 oranges, sliced into half-moons
1 lemon, sliced into rounds or
half-moons
1 lime, sliced into rounds or
half-moons
1 1/2 cups light rum (or to taste)

1/2 cup sugar
1 cup orange juice
1 bottle dry red wine (e.g.,
Merlot or Cabernet
Sauvignon)

◆ Place orange, lemon and lime slices in a large pitcher. In a medium bowl, whisk together rum and sugar until sugar is mostly dissolved; add to pitcher. Pour orange juice and red wine into pitcher, stir with a wooden spoon and adjust sweetness to taste. Let sangria sit for at least 30 minutes before serving to allow flavors to mingle.

DISSOLVING SUGAR
◆ ◆ ◆ ◆ ◆

Help sugar dissolve faster in cold drinks by using a whisk (instead of a wooden spoon) to vigorously stir. Or, start by adding just a bit of liquid to the sugar and stirring to partially dissolve, then add the rest of the liquid and mix until combined.

If you prefer, you can substitute quick-dissolving superfine sugar (AKA bar sugar) to taste in your drink recipes. You can find superfine sugar in the supermarket, or make your own by pulsing regular sugar in the food processor for about 15 seconds.

⋉◆⋊ Fresh Lemonade

Sweet and refreshing lemonade is an ideal treat for a sunny day. But don't bother with the store-bought brands—this homemade version can be made in minutes. Adjust the sugar to taste and skip the chilling time by pouring the lemonade into glasses filled with ice. ℗ **Makes about 7 cups**

1/2 cup sugar
1/2 cup fresh lemon juice

6–7 cups cold water

◆ Add sugar and lemon juice to a large pitcher and vigorously whisk together until sugar is mostly dissolved, about 2 minutes. Add 6 cups of water and whisk again to combine. Taste and add additional water if desired. Cover and chill for two hours, or until cold.

VARIATIONS: Stir in 1/4 cup mint leaves; add 1/4 cup sliced strawberries; substitute some of the lemon juice with lime juice; or make an Arnold Palmer by pouring a glass of half lemonade and half iced tea.

✣◆✣ Chai Hot Chocolate

Cozy up with a friend, a movie and a steaming mug of this decadent drink. This recipe easily doubles—or triples—if you're serving additional people. **D** **Serves 2**

⟫**TIP** *Cocoa powder is made when cocoa butter is removed from chocolate liquor, and the remaining solids are processed into a rich, slightly bitter powder. In the store, always look for unsweetened cocoa powder—either "natural" or the milder "Dutch process"—that contains no added sugars or fillers.*

2 cups milk
3 tablespoons cocoa powder
2 tablespoons sugar, agave
    nectar or maple syrup
1/2 teaspoon cinnamon

1/4 teaspoon ginger powder
1 medium cinnamon stick
4 cardamom pods, cracked
1/2 teaspoon whole black
    peppercorns, cracked

◆ Combine all ingredients in a medium saucepan. Slowly bring to a simmer over medium-low heat, stirring frequently until milk is hot and fragrant, about 8–10 minutes. Remove from heat and steep for a few minutes. Strain and pour into mugs.

◀ *Chai Hot Chocolate*

❖❖❖ MENU IDEAS

POWER BREAKFAST Ⓓ
- Cardamom-Scented Oatmeal
  or Greek Yogurt and Berry Parfait
- *both served with*
  Granola with Tahini

LAZY SUNDAY BRUNCH Ⓓ
- Blueberry Cornmeal Pancakes
  or Challah French Toast with Pear Compote
- Horseradish Omelet
  or Mushroom, Leek and Cheese Strata
- Salsa and Cheddar Home Fries
- Pomegranate Mimosa
- *coffee, tea, orange juice*

LUNCH AT THE OFFICE Ⓓ Ⓟ
- Hard-Boiled Sandwich
- Warm Barley, Apple and Feta Salad *(also tastes great cold)*
  or Orzo and Pinto Bean Salad

KIDS' SCHOOL LUNCH Ⓓ
- *Thermos:* Tuscan Tomato Soup
- Hummus Sandwich Two Ways
  or Carrot, Black Bean and Feta Pita
- Almond Butter Chocolate Chip Cookies
- *baby carrots, bell pepper slices, piece of fruit*

DINNER IN NO-TIME Ⓜ
- Simple Pea Soup with Leeks (optional)
- Miso Ginger Chicken
- Braised Fennel
- *jasmine rice; a simple salad with* Lime Dressing
- Broiled Grapefruit with Brown Sugar

SOUP FOR DINNER Ⓓ Ⓟ
- Drunken Chili
  or Mushroom Lentil Soup
- *crusty bread*
- Moroccan Orange and Olive Salad
- Chocolate Pomegranate Gushers

SALAD FOR DINNER Ⓜ
one bunch of fresh mint does double duty in this meal
- Cucumber and Mint-Spiced Lamb Salad
- Couscous with Dried Cherries and Mint
- Lemon Lime Squares *(use margarine)*

COZY WINTER DINNER Ⓓ
- Sweet and Crunchy Salad
- Thyme-Roasted Root Vegetables
- Ricotta-Stuffed Shells
- Glazed Cinnamon Oatmeal Cookies

LIGHT SPRING DINNER Ⓓ

- Spinach and Sweet Pea Soup
- Asparagus and Avocado Salad
- Tilapia Four Ways
- Strawberries and Cream with
  Toasted Hazelnuts
  or Rhubarb Sauce *over ice cream*

REFRESHING SUMMER DINNER Ⓜ

- Peach and Tomato Salad
- Grilled Herbed Potatoes
- Grilled Lamb Chops with Mint
  Chimichurri
- Watermelon Ice Pops
  or Summer Crumble

HEARTY FALL DINNER Ⓜ

- Sweet Potato Kale Soup with
  White Beans
- Sesame Seed Chicken Cutlets
- Pan-Roasted Brussels Sprouts with
  Toasted Almonds
- Maple Baked Pears

MIDDLE EASTERN-INSPIRED DINNER Ⓓ

- Israeli Caprese Salad
- White Bean Hummus with
  Frizzled Shallots
- Shakshuka
- *crusty bread or pita*
- Malabi with Pistachios

VEGETARIAN FRIENDLY DINNER Ⓓ

- Ginger Sesame Baked Tempeh
- Garlicky Sautéed Greens
- Caramelized Onion Rice
- Brownies with Pomegranate
  Whipped Cream

PIZZA NIGHT Ⓓ

- Tart and Creamy Salad
- Artichoke, Pesto and Black Olive Pizza
- Spinach, Peppers and Mozzarella Pizza
- Orange Floats

SIMPLE BUT ELEGANT DINNER PARTY Ⓓ

- Ricotta and Pistachio Stuffed Figs
  and/or Apple Butter Cheddar Toasts
- Tart and Creamy Salad
- Lemony Asparagus
- Colcannon
- Citrus Cod with White Wine
- Raspberry Cheesecake in a Jar
  or Cinnamon Chocolate Pudding

BACKYARD BARBECUE Ⓜ

- Cumin and Cilantro Burgers
  or Dried Cherry Burgers
  and/or Portobello Burgers *(omit cheese)*
- Basil Two-Bean Salad
- Lemony Pasta Salad
- Sunshine Sangria
- Grilled Pineapple with Minted
  Raspberry Smash

GAME NIGHT SNACK SPREAD Ⓓ Ⓟ

- Souped-Up Deviled Eggs
- Spicy Black Bean Spread
- Guacamole with Chopped Egg
- *corn chips or pita chips*
- Rum and Ginger Cocktails

MOVIE NIGHT Ⓓ

- Parmesan Popcorn
  or Crispy Roasted Chickpeas
- Mocha Shortbread Cookies
- Chai Hot Chocolate
  or Fresh Lemonade

❧◆❧ INGREDIENT SOURCES

The resources here will help you find great fresh produce, specialty ingredients and sustainably produced kosher meat, cheese, chocolate and other grocery items. Cooking—and eating!—kosher and ethically has never been so easy for the home chef.

❧ FRUITS / VEGETABLES

DIRECTORY OF FRUIT STANDS
AND FARMERS' MARKETS
www.fruitstands.com

DIRECTORY OF COMMUNITY
SUPPORTED AGRICULTURE (CSA)
PROGRAMS
www.localharvest.org

HAZON'S JEWISH CSA LOCATIONS
www.hazon.org/CSA

❧ SPICES

PEREG GOURMET SPICES
www.pereg-spices.com

THE SPICE HOUSE
www.thespicehouse.com

❧ MEAT / POULTRY

The following companies merge ecological sustainability and humane animal treatment with *kashrut*. Many of these companies are new and expanding all the time. Visit their Web sites to find up-to-date information.

GOLDEN WEST CATTLE COMPANY
Steaks, Beef and Pickled Meats
www.goldenwestglatt.biz

GROW AND BEHOLD FOODS
Poultry
www.growandbehold.com

KOL FOODS
Poultry, Beef and Lamb
www.kolfoods.com

NESHAMA GOURMET KOSHER FOODS
*Chicken, Turkey and Beef Sausage;
Kosher Organic Chicken Sausage*
www.neshama.us

RED HEIFER FARM
Chicken, Beef
www.redheiferfarm.com

WISE ORGANIC PASTURES
Chicken, Turkey and Beef
www.wiseorganicpastures.com

CHEESE

5-SPOKE CREAMERY
Artisanal Jack and Cheddar
www.5spokecreamery.com

CABOT CREAMERY
Kosher Cheddar
www.shopcabot.com

LES PETITES FERMIERES
*Brie, Camembert, Gouda, Cheddar,
Fontina, Harvarti and more…*
www.aifoods.com/Les_Petites_Fermieres.html

REDWOOD HILL FARM
*Goat Cheddar, Fresh Goat Cheese
(chevre), Feta and Yogurt*
www.redwoodhill.com

SUGAR RIVER CHEESE
Cheddar, Jack and Parmesan
www.sugarrivercheese.com

TILLAMOOK
Kosher Cheddar
www.tillamookcheese.com

VERMONT BUTTER & CHEESE CREAMERY
*Crème Fraiche, Cultured Butter,
Mascarpone, Fromage Blanc, Quark*
www.vermontcreamery.com

GOURMET GROCERY

GOURMET FOOD STORE (SEARCH "KOSHER")
www.gourmetfoodstore.com

IMAGINE FOODS
*Organic Vegetable Broth and
Pareve Chicken Broth*
www.imaginefoods.com

SADAF
*Pomegranate Molasses and
Other Middle Eastern products*
www.sadaf.com

CHOCOLATE

CHOCOLOVE
www.chocolove.com

EQUAL EXCHANGE
www.equalexchange.coop

GHIRADELLI
www.ghirardelli.com

LAKE CHAMPLAIN CHOCOLATES
www.lakechamplainchocolates.com

SUNSPIRE
www.sunspire.com

PAREVE ICE CREAM

COCONUT BLISS
www.coconutbliss.com

TRADER JOE'S SOY CREAMY
www.traderjoes.com

Measurement Conversion Chart

❧ APPROXIMATE EQUIVALENTS

1 stick butter = 8 tablespoons = 1/4 cup

1 cup all-purpose presifted flour or dried breadcrumbs = 5 ounces

1 cup granulated sugar = 8 ounces

1 cup packed brown sugar = 6 ounces

1 cup confectioners' sugar = 4 1/2 ounces

1 cup honey or syrup = 12 ounces

1 cup grated cheese = 4 ounces

1 cup dried beans = 6 ounces

1 large egg yolk = about 2 ounces or 3 tablespoons

1 egg white = about 2 tablespoons

❧ LIQUID CONVERSIONS

U.S.	IMPERIAL	METRIC
2 tablespoons	1 fluid ounce	30 milliliters
3 tablespoons	1 1/2 fluid ounces	45 milliliters
1/4 cup	2 fluid ounces	60 milliliters
1/3 cup	2 1/2 fluid ounces	75 milliliters
1/3 cup + 1 tablespoon	3 fluid ounces	90 milliliters
1/3 cup + 2 tablespoons	3 1/2 fluid ounces	100 milliliters
1/2 cup	4 fluid ounces	125 milliliters
2/3 cup	5 fluid ounces	150 milliliters
3/4 cup	6 fluid ounces	175 milliliters
3/4 cup + 2 tablespoons	7 fluid ounces	200 milliliters
1 cup	8 fluid ounces	250 milliliters
1 cup + 2 tablespoons	9 fluid ounces	275 milliliters
1 1/4 cups	10 fluid ounces	300 milliliters
1 1/3 cups	11 fluid ounces	325 milliliters
1 1/2 cups	12 fluid ounces	350 milliliters
1 2/3 cups	13 fluid ounces	375 milliliters
1 3/4 cups	14 fluid ounces	400 milliliters
1 3/4 cups + 2 tablespoons	15 fluid ounces	450 milliliters
2 cups (1 pint)	16 fluid ounces	500 milliliters
2 1/2 cups	20 fluid ounces (1 pint)	600 milliliters
3 3/4 cups	1 1/2 pints	900 milliliters
4 cups	1 3/4 pints	1 liter

❧ WEIGHT CONVERSIONS

U.S.	METRIC
1/2 ounce	15 grams
1 ounce	30 grams
1 1/2 ounce	45 grams
2 ounces	60 grams
2 1/2 ounces	75 grams
3 ounces	90 grams
3 1/2 ounces	100 grams
4 ounces	125 grams
5 ounces	150 grams
6 ounces	175 grams
7 ounces	200 grams
8 ounces	250 grams
9 ounces	275 grams
10 ounces	300 grams
11 ounces	325 grams
12 ounces	350 grams
13 ounces	375 grams
14 ounces	400 grams
15 ounces	450 grams
1 pound	500 grams

❧ OVEN TEMPERATURES

FAHRENHEIT	CELSIUS
250	120
275	140
300	150
325	160
350	180
375	190
400	200
425	220
450	230
475	240
500	260

Reduce the temperature by 20 degrees Celsius or 68 degrees Fahrenheit if using a fan-assisted oven.

PAREVE Ⓟ